UNDER THE MIDNIGHT SUN

Journey with the Sahtu Dene

Mary-Anne Neal

UNDER THE MIDNIGHT SUN
Journey with the Sahtu Dene

ISBN: 978-1-928114-33-8 (paperback)
978-1-928114-34-5 (e-book)

Cover photo: *Late evening sun over Colville Lake, NWT* by Mary-Anne Neal
All photos by the author unless otherwise noted.

☯ Reciprocity Publishing, Victoria BC Canada
Design: Daniel Doherty

Dedication

This book is dedicated to the Dene heart, beating strong throughout the North, and to the Sahtu Dene who accepted me and believed in me. We found your voice and published four fascinating *Dene Heroes of the Sahtu* books written in your own words to honour the Dene spirit. Together, we are all stronger. Serving you has been my great joy and I miss all of you, every day of my life.

You have to live it to learn it.

Chief Wilbert Kochon
Behdzi Ah'da First Nation

Acknowledgments

This book is not mine alone. The moving force behind every endeavour is the team. I owe a huge debt of gratitude to people who encouraged me to tell the story of my remarkable journey with the Dene. Special thanks are due to the band leaders of Colville Lake for their wise counsel: David Codzi, Wilbert Kochon and Joseph Kochon (Tarzelaw).

Thank you to the Dene and non-Dene who reviewed parts of the book and gave me the opportunity to clarify my thoughts. You know who you are.

Thank you to all the Fort Franklin (Deline) fishing guides at Trophy Lodge in 1971, now grown men with families of their own. You gave me laughter when I needed it most.

Thank you to the Dene who quietly demonstrate heroic qualities – you are role models for all of us. Heartfelt thanks to the Sahtu men and women who warmly welcomed me into their homes and freely shared their experiences and knowledge.

Thank you to all the people in our human family who continue to fight for social justice, especially those who are dedicated to restoring our Indigenous brothers and sisters to their rightful place of honour in our society.

Mahsi ... mahsi cho!

Contents

It's impossible, said Pride.
It's risky, said Experience.
It's pointless, said Reason.
Give it a try, whispered the Heart.

Author unknown

Preface

This book is a tribute to the Dene (*deh nay*) people who welcomed me as a teenager into their communities half a century ago and then again, as a grandmother, in 2015. It is also an attempt to make sense of the jumbled hodgepodge of events and people that form a significant part of my life. I'm not sure I am able to impose any kind of order on the chaos of my life, especially the transformative events that occurred during the summer of 1971. But I'll try. Because what happened to my soul in the far North shaped my adult life and still drives my passion for social justice. Reconnecting with the Dene people proves how deeply those strands are woven into the fabric of their and my existence.

Life is so strange and mysterious that it easily defeats my attempt to corral it within the borders of the written page. Still, that pivotal summer remains not just in my memory but also in the memories of the Sahtu Dene people. My presence in their communities had a profound impact. At a personal level, a budding romance was destroyed when two lives were ripped apart because of racial prejudice. Today, our souls have reconnected. I share a bond with the Dene that turned out to be unbreakable. The people of the Sahtu embraced me, an outsider, as one of their own. Our story is as simple as that and yet so much more.

I could have romanticized my summer experience; instead, I buried the painful events that culminated in my leaving the North long ago. Shutting out the memories, I tried to forget that the adventure had ever happened. Embarrassment about my behaviour gradually melted into a quiet sadness deep within my soul. Eventually, the line between real and imagined began to blur as the details faded.

Scattered moments from that summer occasionally rose to the surface and haunted my dreams. As I moved through life – getting married, having children, embarking on a career, travelling the world – a little bit of my heart remained with the

Dene of the Sahtu. When the pieces of the puzzle finally came together after more than four decades, I was surprised to discover the truth about what had really happened. I learned that my dismissal from the fishing lodge was not solely due to inappropriate alcohol consumption; the interplay of racism and young adult hormones had a lot to do with it. Maybe I had just been a pawn in a complex game of chess that played out on the tundra under the glare of the midnight sun.

Some details from my teenage years are understandably foggy, but certain moments shine with crystal clarity. Thankfully, I kept an extensive diary during the summer of 1971. People I have since reconnected with added accuracy and verified events that I was unaware of at the time. Dene friends also clarified the ambiguity and unspoken questions that played in my mind.

I hope my observations are received as respectfully as I intend them to be.

Mary-Anne Neal

Late evening sun over Colville Lake, NWT (mid-September).

Sahtu Region
Northwest Territories
Canada

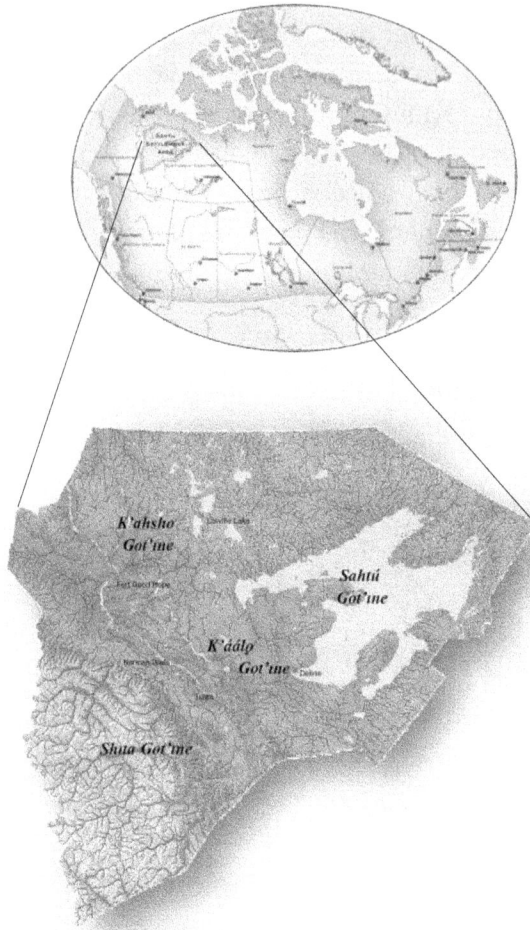

Map courtesy of the *Sahtu Atlas*, GIS Project, GNWT.

1   In the Beginning

The drone of the Cessna Caravan lulls me into a half-sleep and I find myself beginning to doze off. Eyes closed, I drift back in time 45 years. My spirit floats back to that unforgettable summer when I left a piece of my heart with the Dene people in the high Arctic under the midnight sun. It's 1971. I am 19 years old again, aboard a Cessna 180, en route to the most remote community in North America – Colville Lake, north of the Arctic Circle, in the Sahtu region of Canada's Northwest Territories.

*

The only way I can think of to tell this story is exactly how it happened from my perspective. Although it still seems like a dream, writing about the experience might capture the essence of those months that I spent in the Arctic when I was aging out of my teen years.

At 19, I was blissfully doubt-free and certain that things would work out regardless of the predicaments I created for myself. An unshakeable faith in human nature took me to an isolated bush camp in the far North, where a summer-long encounter with the Dene people changed the trajectory of my life. I continue to feel the ripples of that experience even now, at the age of 69.

I grew up in Edmonton, Alberta, known then as Canada's 'Gateway to the North.' As a little girl growing up in the 1950s, I earnestly believed in social justice. All I really wanted to do was to bring happiness to others. I especially loved looking after babies and toddlers. The idea of missionary work with underprivileged children was enormously appealing. Maybe I could become a nun? Working to make the world a better place, learning foreign languages, feeding hungry infants, understanding different cultures – these are the yearnings that drove me. Over the years, however, the usual teenage temptations got in the way. I loved to party, flirt with boys and go out on dates. I also spent an inordinate amount of time studying so that I would make my parents proud once I attended university. Needless to say, I did not dedicate my life to the convent. A sometimes-reckless sense of adventure got me into trouble from time to time, though I usually emerged unscathed.

Excelling at schoolwork was my goal throughout my school years. Outstanding achievement was rewarded with 'H' for Honours on a report card, and every kid in the Gillese family was determined to earn straight *Hs* in every subject. I rarely spoke up in class, but I listened alertly to my teachers, read avidly and did not hesitate to ask questions. Only the social studies teachers found my interruptions annoying, possibly because they were unable to answer my questions about the First People of North America: "What were their names?" "How did they learn to speak French and English?" And, looking around at my white, Anglo-Saxon classmates, "Where are the native people now?" I failed to understand why so little of the school curriculum was devoted to the people who originally inhabited the land we now call Canada. Those unresolved questions lingered in my mind and later became the catalyst for my teenaged quest to find answers.

My father and his family immigrated from Ireland in 1926. In this 1931 photo on the homestead, he is 11 years old.

My father was a writer whose life journey took him in fascinating directions. Although he had achieved some local and even national fame through his publications, Dad earned barely enough to feed and house a large family – six children, his ailing mother and an adopted child from war-torn El Salvador. A devout Catholic, John Patrick Gillese[1] supported the Oblates of Mary Immaculate (OMI), and we often hosted Oblate missionaries at our sprawling home in Edmonton. The capital city of Alberta, Edmonton grew quickly in the 1960s, fed by the oil boom and U.S. mineral exploration money. My preference was always country living, so I fled the city whenever I could find a ride out to either of my grandparents' farms – one located to the north of the city and the other to the south.

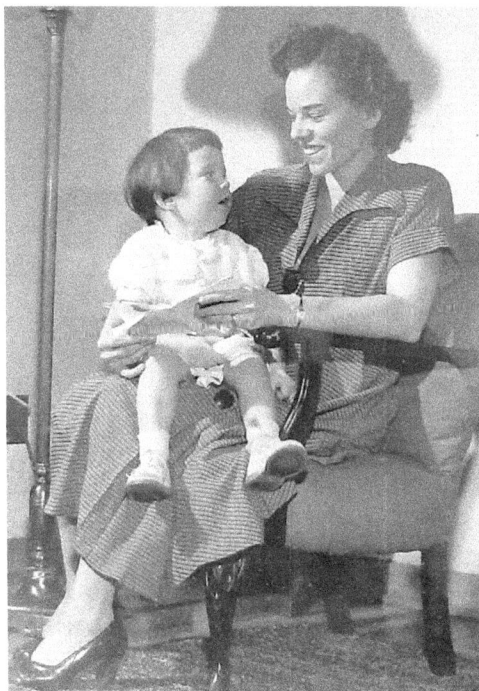

I am three years old in this 1955 photo with my mom in our family home.

_____

[1] Author, editor and mentor to emerging authors

I admired the OMI priests who are dedicated to serving people in need. These missionaries work in communities that request their assistance, responding to the wishes of the people and building skills that will improve living conditions. The OMI mandate is to safeguard human dignity, foster harmony, strive for social justice and promote a culture of peace – the same values that I so fervently believed in.

I am on my way to church with my Irish grandmother, ready to receive my First Holy Communion in 1958.

Imagine my delight when I came home one day in 1969 to learn that our family would be hosting a visitor from one of the most inaccessible communities in Canada's far North. My dad told me that I was going to meet a talented man with an unsurpassed work ethic, great courage, compassion and a zest for life. Father Bernard Brown, OMI, served the First People in the Arctic, referring to them as *Indians*.[2] The people he worked with were known as the *Hareskin Dene* (*deh nay*). *Dene* means 'people' in their language, now called North Slavey by linguists. Alexander Mackenzie, the first European to explore the Northwest Territories, referred to the original inhabitants of the land as Hareskin Indians because their clothing was made of rabbit skin. The Hareskin Dene are also known as the 'End of the Earth' people because only the Inuit live further north of the Dene territory. Father Brown lived in a tiny Dene community nestled on the shores of Colville Lake, north of the Arctic Circle and far from any other settlements.

Living in harmony with nature for thousands of years, the Dene still followed the natural rhythms of the seasons. Dene families moved within a vast territory, erecting encampments in various places where they stayed for a few months at a time. Colville Lake, originally called *Dela Gotine* (the gathering place), had long been a favourite spot because caribou were plentiful and the lake teemed with fish.

The fiercely independent Hareskin people had established a semi-permanent encampment on the shores of Colville Lake at the place where they set their ptarmigan nets (*Kah Bah Mi Tue* in their language). A few log cabins housed the Dene men, women and children who gathered seasonally to hunt, trap and fish in the area. In 1961, Father Brown acquired permission from the diocesan bishop to establish a mission at Colville Lake. Enlisting help from the people who already lived there, Father Brown directed construction of Our Lady of the Snows parish. Funding from the Vatican enabled him to hire and train locals to erect a church, build a dock on the lake and hammer together some buildings from local timber.

By the time I first met Father Brown at our home in 1969, the tiny mission was thriving. I was 17 years old, finishing high school and living with my family in Edmonton. Father Brown

---

[2] The terms 'Indian' or 'native' were in common usage until the beginning of the 21st century; they are now referred to collectively as First People.

hailed from Rochester, New York, and the lengthy travel required for his rare visits home included a two-day stopover in Edmonton. Father Brown had flown his Cessna 180 from Colville Lake to Norman Wells, where he refuelled. From Norman Wells, he flew to Yellowknife, where he spent another night. Then he boarded a commercial aircraft for a flight to Edmonton. Because my parents were staunch supporters of the Oblates of Mary Immaculate, Dad had invited Father Brown to stay with our family for a few days as the missionary priest made his way south. After the Edmonton stopover, the priest would continue his long journey from the Arctic Circle to New York state.

In 1969, the year I first met Father Brown, I was 17 years old and attending Archbishop MacDonald High School in Edmonton, Alberta.

I accompanied Dad to the airport, where he greeted Father Brown like an old friend. I had forgotten that the missionary

14

had stayed with our family many times over the years. Father Brown remembered me as a little girl, but I only dimly recalled the tall figure who shook my hand. Sitting in the back seat of our 1963 Chevrolet on the way home, I listened as the men reminisced. Father Brown was born in 1920, the same year as my father. Both men both loved the outdoors and they jovially swapped stories about hunting, trapping and fishing.

Later that night, as my mother and I served dinner to Dad and our guest, I eavesdropped again on the men's conversation. Snippets of their dialogue captivated me.

"Shot a couple of caribou the other day and got enough meat to last a few months ... Du Pont gave me an aircraft so I can get around faster ... trained my dog team to haul logs for the buildings ... moose hide mittens ... the language has tones and sounds that we don't have in English ... Dogrib Indians ... Hareskins ..." Father Brown's colourful depiction of bush life with the original inhabitants of the land piqued my curiosity and revived my passion for social justice. Maybe I could finally meet the First People of Canada who had eluded me for so long?

As a child, my imagination had been fuelled by Jack London's books, particularly *Call of the Wild* and *White Fang*. London's vivid descriptions of the North enthralled me and awakened some kind of primal instinct. I envisioned living in the wilderness with only the sky and my sled dogs for companionship. The native people of Colville Lake might have the answers to my questions about their culture and heritage. Father Brown's words fired my spirits because the people he described seemed to share the same longings that I felt. This man was living the life I had dreamed about ever since I was a little girl.

I wanted to know more, to talk to the native people themselves and to learn their story in their own words. I wanted to reach out my hand in friendship so that I might understand how native people think, knowing that their perspective would be radically different from my narrow seventeen-year-old privileged white view of life. I wanted to learn the native language, make friends with the native people, play with their children and immerse myself in their culture and traditions. Maybe I could even haul water for them or help them with their daily chores?

During dinner, Father Brown continued to regale us with stories of life in the Arctic. I listened intently and decided to ask my mom's advice about an idea that was beginning to take shape in my mind.

"Mom, I really want to go up North and visit Father Brown." I was washing the supper dishes while my mother dried them.

"All you need to do is ask," Mom responded with a smile. "It can't hurt to talk to him."

I had always been introverted, more comfortable observing and listening than speaking. So it took all the courage I could muster to approach Father Brown after dinner. He and Dad had moved to the living room where they were seated across from each other, smoking companionably and talking about clairvoyance. I heard the two men mention Jeane Dixon, Edgar Cayce and other people who claim to have powers of extra-sensory perception. My dad relaxed in his easy chair, smoking a cigarette while Father Brown sat on our overstuffed green couch, puffing on a cigar.

"Excuse me ... sorry to interrupt ... I've always wanted to work with underprivileged people," I began hesitantly. Father Brown was intent on his stogie. He exhaled a huge blue-white cloud and looked at me through the haze with piercing hazel eyes. "Go on."

"Well ... " Deep breath. "I wanted to be a nun, but I've kind of decided against it. And I really want to get to know the people you work with. The native people were already living in Canada when people like us arrived, so they have been here for a long time. And your work sounds wonderful. You're living close to nature and sharing their way of life."

"What's your point?" asked Father Brown.

"Could I come and visit you? Get to know the people in Colville Lake? Maybe help you?"

Father Brown looked away from me. He took his cigar out of his mouth, gazed at the smoke curling from it and then looked back at my face. A smile played around his lips; I could see that he was thinking. Finally, the missionary priest spoke.

"If you can get to Colville Lake, I'll give you a place to stay."

My grin spread from ear to ear. Finally I would have a chance to get to know people who had lived in the North since long before settlers arrived. Maybe I could learn their language. Maybe I could become friends with them. Getting to know the native people in the Arctic would be the adventure of a lifetime!

Minutes later, my hopes were dashed. Seeing the look of delight on my face, Father Brown shook his head. He looked at my dad wryly and then spoke to me again.

"You don't have a clue, do you?" Father Brown chuckled, but there was no humour in his voice when he spoke. "There are no roads to Colville Lake. There is no river that runs past Colville Lake. The only way to get to Colville Lake is by air. And the only planes that fly in are privately chartered. They cost a hell of a lot of money. Pretty sure you don't have the cash to get to Colville Lake."

The priest's hazel eyes had gone cold. Then he looked away from me and went back to smoking his cigar. I left Father Brown and my dad quietly murmuring together. Cheeks burning, I made my way upstairs to my bedroom. Now that I knew my dream would never come true, my heart ached with bitter disappointment. My evening prayers were an anguished call for direction in my life.

After that uncomfortable exchange with our visitor, I found it hard to carry on a light-hearted conversation with Father Brown. I was respectful of him as a guest in our house but I kept a wary distance. It was easier for me to spend more time in the kitchen preparing meals than in the dining room serving Dad and our visitor. The following summer, when the OMI missionary visited us again, he remembered our conversation and teased me about it. We were all able to laugh at my childish dreams from the previous year. The memory of his condescending response to my innocent question still rankled but I kept my feelings to myself and was always courteous.

Over the next year, I spent as little time as possible at home, chafing at the confines of my family's two-story stucco house. 1970 was a whirlwind. Dating, attending university classes, studying and writing essays kept me fully occupied all day and most of the night. Since I had earned the highest grade in Alberta on the Grade 12 English 30 provincial examination, my friends and family assumed I would be a writer. I was not so sure. Instead, I wanted to study the First People of Canada. Due to the *Indian Act*, Indigenous Canadians were referred to as *Indians*. The term didn't seem right to me. Why did everyone persist in using an outdated term like that? I thought they should be called 'Original People.' But a teenager like me couldn't possibly change a habit that had been around for at least two hundred years.

Through anthropology and history courses at the University of Alberta, I learned about colonialism and the horrific injustices perpetrated on Indigenous people throughout North America. Once again, I felt a searing sense of obligation to the original inhabitants of Canada, who had been mistreated, ignored and abused for centuries. I immersed myself in learning about Canada's First People. Much of the information came from Franz Boas, who studied the Kwagiulth [spellings vary] people on Canada's West Coast in the early 1900s.

My first year anthropology class was a big eye-opener, especially reading *The Unjust Society*, Harold Cardinal's stinging rebuttal of the federal government's 1969 *White Paper*. Formally known as the *Statement of the Government of Canada on Indian Policy*, the *White Paper* called for assimilation of

Canada's First People. The idea was that the dominant, non-Indigenous culture is superior to Indigenous culture, so native people should simply adopt Eurocentric norms. Publication of the *White Paper* caused an outcry among Indigenous Canadians; eventually the report was revoked. I admired Harold Cardinal for his powerful stance against injustice and his advocacy for Indigenous Canadians.

I couldn't finish reading *Bury My Heart at Wounded Knee*, by Dee Brown, because my tears blurred the words on the pages. Closing the book, I wept openly. My heart grieved for the cruelty suffered by our native brothers and sisters at the hands of government workers, soldiers, settlers and other colonizers. How could I possibly remedy the situation? Clearly an eighteen-year-old university student had nothing to offer except a willing heart. I longed for a sense of purpose but had no direction. My goal was simple .... get to know the First People of the land, support them in any ways that I could and maybe, just maybe, figure out what I wanted to do with my life.

As a way to pay for my university tuition fees, I held numerous part-time jobs. A temporary position with the federal Department of Transportation at the Edmonton Industrial Airport[3] just after my birthday early in 1971 changed my life irrevocably and provided an unexpected ticket to my sojourn with the Dene in Colville Lake.

The university year ended in April and I was working part-time for the Canadian Department of Transportation until mid-May, 1971. At the airport, I was responsible for surveying pilots as they arrived in Edmonton, often after a long journey from a remote outpost in the far North. The young men were invariably surprised to see a leggy nineteen-year-old with long auburn hair dashing across the tarmac to greet them when they

---

[3] Known colloquially as the Downtown Airport or Edmonton Municipal Airport, it closed in 2013.

landed their planes. Meeting the pilots was fun and I couldn't resist flirting with the handsome ones.

One of the pilots I interviewed, a tall, blonde American named John Cesnik, was clearly smitten with me. John was studying to become a doctor. During the summer months, he flew up North to earn enough money to pay for his university tuition. I thought the young man was kind of cute, so I accepted his invitation to accompany him to his cousin's wedding at a hotel on Kingsway Avenue on Saturday night. We danced and celebrated all evening long. I liked John's sweet, trusting nature, though I was not attracted romantically to the crew-cut, blue-eyed pilot. Leaving the crowded ballroom, I was grateful for a cool evening breeze. My date tried to kiss me good night when we said good-bye at my parents' back door, but he had to be content with a peck on my freckled cheek as I squirmed away from his embrace.

Back at the airport on Monday morning, I spent my last day of work as usual – running downstairs from the control tower out on to the runway to greet the pilots and ask them the requisite questions for the Department of Transportation (DOT). As I filled out the surveys, I realized that one of the biggest challenges facing a bush pilot is the high-altitude solitude, specifically the possibility of falling asleep while flying the plane. Auto pilot is on, the engines are droning, and the scenery is unchanging for hours. Suddenly the penny dropped, and I had a flash of insight. I only weighed a little over a hundred pounds and I could carry a conversation. Maybe I could tag along as excess baggage on a bush plane heading north. A long flight in a tiny plane can be dangerously boring, especially for a pilot flying solo. Best to have some company to keep monotony at bay. Right?

I suggested the plan to John that afternoon. Without hesitation, the young pilot agreed that I could accompany him on the lengthy, tedious trip to Yellowknife the following day in his Piper Cherokee. I think my new friend hoped that spending time together would thaw my feelings toward him.

Well, there's always a chance, I guess. Regardless, I was thrilled with his response. "Yay! I'm going up North!" I was buoyed by the thought, sensing that I was on the threshold of a life-changing experience.

This would be my first long trip in an airplane. It would take us more than four hours in John's tiny aircraft to fly almost 1,000 miles[4] (1600 kilometres) due north of Edmonton. I didn't know what to expect in the North, but I knew it was going to be a grand adventure. Since there were no phones in Colville Lake and the postal service was unreliable, we had no way to reach Father Brown and let him know I was on my way. It had been two years since our conversation about the possibility of visiting him. I would just have to arrive on his doorstep and hope that he remembered his long-ago promise to host me if I managed to make it all the way to Colville Lake. Fingers crossed!

Now ... what to take? How long would I stay? What would the weather be like? Where might this journey lead me? I could only guess what to anticipate in the coming months. "Be sure to pack warm clothes," Mom called to me. "Make some ham sandwiches to eat on the plane." She and Dad were happy they would have one less mouth to feed.

I pulled out my new, robins-egg blue suitcase from the closet. Bought in the hope of travelling beyond the prairies one day, the little rectangular bag was soft-sided and small enough for me to carry comfortably in one hand. From my limited clothing supply, it took only a few minutes to pick out two changes of clothes and a warm jacket. I would wear jeans and a T-shirt most of the time, with shorts and a navy-blue sleeveless top for hot days. A long-sleeved sweater for colder weather, an extra pair of socks and a change of underwear completed my wardrobe. I would soon regret neglecting to pack insect repellant.

---

[4] Canada employed the imperial system of measurement until the metric system was introduced in the mid-1970s.

Everything I needed for an indefinite period of time north of the Arctic Circle didn't begin to fill the tiny blue suitcase. I tucked in two *Oh Henry!*® chocolate bars for me and John to snack on along the way. My thin wallet held a $20 bill, a $10 bill, a $5 bill and three $1 bills. Will $38 be enough to keep me going? No time to go to the bank, so the small amount of cash will have to suffice. No credit card. No cell phone. No camera. No GPS. Not even a map. My only identification was a recently acquired driver's license. I would have to remember to wind my wristwatch every day so that I could keep track of time.

When I fell into bed that night, I asked my guardian angel 'to light, to guard, to rule and guide'[5] me on my way. Nervous anticipation kept me awake until the wee hours of the morning.

---

[5] Angel of God, my guardian dear, to whom God's love entrusts me here, ever this night be at my side, to light, to guard, to rule and guide. Amen.

2   On My Way

Not all who wander are lost.

J.R.R. Tolkien

The next day, May 15, 1971, I said goodbye to my parents and excitedly climbed into the co-pilot's seat of John's single-engine Piper Cherokee. Then we soared northward into the sky. Below me, the city of Edmonton quickly disappeared from view. An orderly patchwork of farms, fences and fields quickly became an unbroken expanse of green – the boreal forest[6] stretched beyond the horizon in all directions. The vast woodland was followed by muskeg, ponds and innumerable lakes that look like giant footsteps from the air. On and on we flew, straight north to Yellowknife, capital city of the Northwest Territories.

The four-hour flight tested my nerves many times. At one point, we hit a thunderstorm. The clouds around our small plane transformed from powdery white to deep purple, black, blue and steel gray. Lightning flashed all around us. The plane dropped twenty feet at a time, and my stomach plummeted along with it. John saw the look on my face and suggested I gnaw on some celery he had brought along. Chewing kept the nausea down, but I still felt sick to my stomach. John had also placed a plastic bucket on the cockpit floor next to my feet in case the sandwiches I had eaten for lunch came back up.

As we neared Yellowknife, the skies cleared and massive Great Slave Lake[7] came into view, snow-covered as far as the eye could see. I briefly wondered why it is named 'Slave Lake,' then turned my attention to the scenery below. The four-billion-year-old Canadian Shield rock formations featured prominently among the low, rolling landscape of bog, willows, spruce and birch trees. I was north of the sixtieth parallel and

---

[6] Also known as the Taiga, it is 50% larger than the Amazonian ecosystem.

[7] The deepest lake in North America at 641 m (2014 feet).

a long way from home. Here, daylight in mid-May lasts almost twenty hours. The enormous sky seemed even bigger and bluer than the familiar Alberta sky.

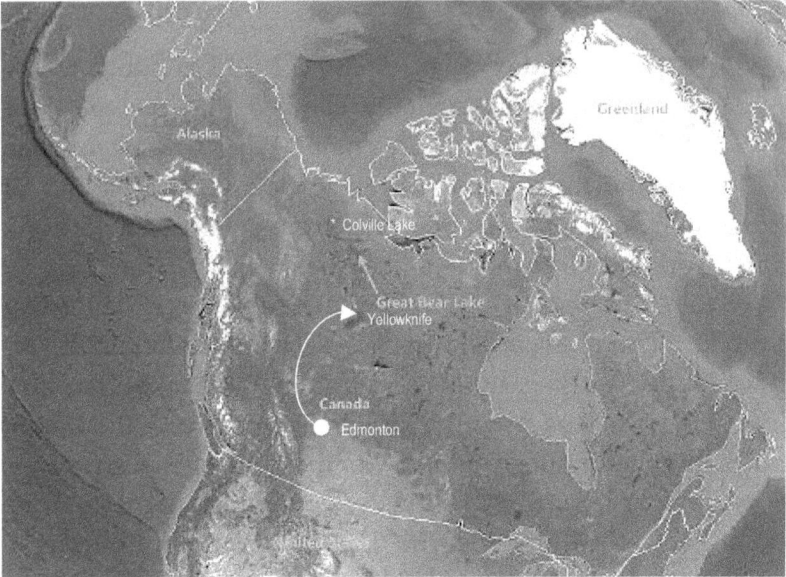

The long flight from Edmonton to Yellowknife brought me halfway to my destination.

Upon arrival in Yellowknife, I realized that I was now at the mercy of fate. I did not know a single soul other than my pilot, who would soon be on his way to the North Pole without me. Pilots, ground crew and mechanics stared at me when we landed and disembarked from the Piper Cherokee. John introduced me to Duncan and Malcolm of Northward Aviation, who sympathized when they heard I was on my way to far-off Colville Lake. But the reality was that no one flew to that inaccessible location unless an organization paid a hefty sum for the flight. The only way to get to Colville Lake was to charter a plane. The $38 in my pocket would not take me far.

My heart sank when I realized that I was less than halfway to my destination. Now I truly depended on the kindness of strangers. In that, I was not disappointed. Dunc and Malcolm offered to take me as far as Norman Wells[8], 500 miles (800 kilometres) northwest of Yellowknife on the Mackenzie River (known to the Dene as the *Deh Cho*). The Northward Aviation crew were hauling cargo to the Wells tomorrow and I was welcome to join them aboard their DC-3. A flight to Norman Wells would bring me one giant step closer to Colville Lake.

Malcolm showed me around Yellowknife, though there wasn't much to see in the recently-incorporated city of 5,000 people – Franklin Avenue, the main street with two traffic lights, a hardware store, a Hudson's Bay Company general store, the Yellowknife Inn, a few crude buildings and a small post office. Malcolm took me for a drive to Old Town, where I saw tiny, brightly painted houses in rainbow colours, tumbledown shacks, privies, a couple of Quonset huts, some trailers and a motley assortment of small businesses catering to trappers and hunters.

Arriving at the lone apartment building in town, Malcolm introduced me to his bachelor friend, Glenn, who kindly allowed me to spend the night on his couch. After just a piece of toast for breakfast the next morning, Glenn escorted me back to the airport, where I climbed aboard Northward Aviation's DC-3 for the three-hour flight to Norman Wells with Dunc and his co-pilot, Brian. During our flight, Dunc pointed out spectacular scenery including the Mackenzie River and towering Bear Rock, just outside of Fort Norman (known once again as *Tulit'a* – where the waters meet – since 1996).

By the time we landed in Norman Wells, all three of us were famished so we walked over to the only restaurant in town. The restaurant looked more like a poorly built barn – simple, unpainted, ramshackle wood frame construction with bare rafters, plywood walls and a dirt floor. About twenty noisy patrons were laughing and chatting at long wooden tables, crowded together on benches and a few rickety chairs.

---

[8] Known to the Dene as *Tlie Gohlini* (where the oil is).

When we arrived in the doorway, conversation ceased. Everyone stopped talking and stared at us.

That's when I noticed that the entire clientele was male. Aside from the waitress, I was the only woman within eyesight. I was suddenly acutely aware that a sleeveless blouse and short blue-jean shorts bared my slender arms and legs. Clearly, the men in the room hadn't seen a young white woman in a long time. I looked down at the floor and quietly followed Dunc and Brian to a table where we sat down across from three other men.

The ruckus started up again once we were seated, and I felt somewhat more comfortable with my companions guarding either side of me. A lone waitress, stringy hair pulled behind her ears, rushed around serving plates of food to the hungry men. Finally, it was our turn. The skinny, middle-aged server strode up to our table and snapped, "Are you having lunch?" Dunc and Brian nodded to her and looked at me. Instead of answering immediately, I asked, "What's for lunch?" The woman glared at me with undisguised animosity. "ARE YOU HAVING LUNCH? OR NOT?" she demanded. "Oh, of course," I said. "Yes, please. Thank you!"

Angrily, the waitress turned on her heel and left the table. A few minutes later, she slapped down an identical plate of food for each of us – a mound of mashed potatoes, a pork chop and some canned peas. I was so hungry that I wolfed down the food. I could tell the waitress hated me. But why?

That night, I stayed with a young married couple, Steve and Terri England. Steve was a pilot and Terri was thrilled to have an overnight guest. We chatted together companionably all evening. Playing with their six-month-old baby in the safety of their little home was a welcome relief from having my guard up around all the men in town.

Terri explained that almost everything in this small Imperial Oil town had been barged in by boat on the Mackenzie River last summer. Barging freight is less expensive than flying it in, but cargo flights such as the one that brought me to town are necessary because the Mackenzie River is frozen for nearly ten months of the year. The town only has one store, operated by Imperial Oil. Terri told me that the shelves are empty except for a few necessities, and the shop is only occasionally open for business.

The next morning, Steve took me to the control tower at the Norman Wells airport. The air traffic controller radioed Father Brown who was already scheduled to fly to Norman Wells to pick up two anthropologists from Cornell University in New York. A lucky break for me! As we waited for Father Brown to arrive, I chatted with Joel and Susan Savishinsky. Joel was actually being paid to study the Hareskin people in Colville Lake as part of his field work for a doctoral degree in anthropology.

The university had hired Father Brown to fly Joel and Susan to and from Colville Lake. Joel agreed that I could accompany them if we could cram all our baggage into the small plane. The newly married couple planned to spend the summer in Colville Lake, researching, observing and photographing the residents. Later, the Savishinskys would publish their findings in *The Western Canadian Journal of Anthropology*. The excitement of these two young scientists was contagious. Only a few years older than me, we shared a common fascination with native people and native culture.

A few hours later, we heard Father Brown's voice crackle over the radio at the control tower. He would land soon. We all watched Father Brown bring his little Cessna 180 down on to the Norman Wells runway. The aircraft bounced three times before rolling to a stop and the air traffic controllers were not impressed. They judge a pilot by the landing; this was not a good one. Still, I was delighted that the final leg of my journey was at hand.

This 1971 Cessna 180 is similar to CF-SLA, Father Brown's plane that carried me to Colville Lake.

Yes, I was delighted, but I was also somewhat apprehensive. How would Father Brown react to the news that I had actually made it this far? Would his offer from two years ago still stand? Should I hug him? Exactly what was I getting myself into?

With a big smile, I ran to Father Brown as he emerged from his Cessna. The look on the man's face told me he was not overjoyed to see me. Our greeting was awkward. Avoiding my outstretched arms, he seemed ill at ease and instead turned his attention to his paying customers, Joel and Susan. Not a good start. Alarm bells were ringing. I began to wonder how we would get along in Colville Lake.

Was I reckless? Inspired? Courageous? Naïve? Or maybe all of the above? My heart had spoken to me and that call had been irresistible. Somehow, I knew that I was about to enter an entirely different world, one that my teenaged mind never could have imagined. I tried to dispel an unsettling sense of foreboding. This adventure was going to take all the courage I could muster.

3   I Arrive

Scrambling into the cockpit of the tiny aircraft, I find a place beside Father Brown in the co-pilot's seat. In addition to his three passengers, Father Brown is picking up much-needed supplies and a large bag of mail addressed to Colville Lake, with envelopes and packages that have been accumulating in Norman Wells for six weeks or longer. Fitting passengers and freight into Father Brown's little Cessna is a tight squeeze. Really glad my soft-sided suitcase easily crushes down to accommodate the more important cargo. The Cessna is so heavily loaded that we need the entire length of the runway before the plane finally becomes airborne.

Our destination lies 140 miles (225 kilometres) northeast of Norman Wells, more than thirty miles north of the Arctic Circle, which is the 66th parallel. Most settlements in the Mackenzie River valley are located on the river or one of its tributaries, but the people of Colville Lake lack a direct water route to their community. This little bush camp can only be reached overland or by plane.

Leaving Norman Wells and the mighty Mackenzie River behind, we fly over awe-inspiring scenery. Although it is mid-May, snow still blankets the ground. The lakes and rivers are frozen over. Then, as we cross the Franklin Mountains, a jaw-dropping precipice below makes me gasp. Breathtaking cliffs, icy lakes, snow-covered trees. Not a sign of any kind of human settlement anywhere – just unbounded tracts of forest and tundra interlaced with thousands of waterways. Endless bush country as far as the eye can see.

The inland Arctic is a vast, intricate labyrinth of muskeg, willows, tundra, bogs, boreal forest, shallow lakes and winding rivers. It seems like a prehistoric world. Seen from above, the lonely landscape appears lifeless but I know that nature flourishes here. Otherwise, how could the people survive? The North is also a land of extremes. Winter temperatures regularly plunge to -60 degrees Fahrenheit (-50 degrees Celsius). Today, the mercury has soared so quickly that snow evaporates into the air without melting. Within a few days of this hot weather, the glacial landscape will be a thing of the past until winter comes again in September. I am in awe of people who continue to make their home in such an inhospitable climate.

An hour and a half later, a glittering expanse of ice indicates that our journey's end is near. My excitement mounts. In 1964, Father Brown had established Our Lady of the Snows mission on the shores of Colville Lake that he now calls home. I have seen pictures of the picturesque log church built by the natives under his direction. Can't wait to see it in person.

We are now far beyond the tree line and the rough, bare tundra stretches in every direction, with low willow bushes and a few stunted shrubs here and there. Little cabins and canvas tents are scattered haphazardly beside the ice-covered lake. No roads, no electricity, no telephones, no post office, no running water, no police – welcome to on-the-land living in Colville Lake.

Father Brown steers the Cessna toward a narrow dirt landing strip on a high point of land. I see people popping out of their tents, waving and running toward the landing strip. Everyone – kids and adults alike – rushes up the hill to meet the airplane. They are speaking an unusual language and they are frankly curious about Father Brown's guests. Strangely, Father Brown is not interacting with them. Aside from a few strong fellows who help us carry the boxes of supplies, he ignores the men, women and children who are clamoring for attention. My host's behaviour is puzzling, a disturbing harbinger of things to come.

The children stare at me, a freckle-faced interloper, with a mixture of fascination and curiosity. Adults seem friendly but guarded. Some speak English slowly, in guttural tones. Hard for me to understand their thickly accented words. Are they welcoming us? Our entourage begins to make its way down the embankment. As we walk down the rocky slope toward the cluster of cabins, a little native girl falls down near us. She has scraped her knee on the gravel and cries out in pain, but Father Brown doesn't even glance at her. I can see that he doesn't want me to stop walking to console the wailing girl. I assumed a missionary would be compassionate towards everyone. The priest's disinterest alarms me, and I begin to wonder: What's wrong with Father Brown? Doesn't he care about the people? I have to step fast to keep up with his long strides.

A fifteen-minute hike past tents, small cabins and snarling sled dogs brings us to Father Brown's enclave – an inviting log home, Our Lady of the Snows church, some cabins, various sheds and outbuildings. All are well-built timber structures, beautifully maintained, neat and tidy. Even the privies are charming miniature replicas of the cabins. Father Brown's residence, church and fishing lodge are remarkable examples of one person's engineering and architectural skill. But he could not have built the settlement without the hard-working native people who were paid $1 an hour to construct the buildings over a three-year period, using only local materials and rudimentary tools.

Lacking even a wheelbarrow or chainsaw, industrious Colville Lake workers hauled rocks, sawed logs and surmounted formidable obstacles to achieve Father Brown's vision. Some of the logs were dragged here by dogsled in the winter from forty miles away, below the tree line. Others were located on the south side of the lake and then floated to the building site during the summer. Constructing a log house requires precise attention to detail and I am soon to learn that Father Brown is a perfectionist in every task he sets for himself and others.

Father Brown's painting 'Our Lady of the Snows' hangs behind the altar in the Colville Lake church.

The native people also live in nicely built cabins, but each home consists of only one room, as opposed to Father Brown's five-room mansion. Their cabins are situated a short walk away from Father Brown's buildings. There is no school or structure of any sort where people might gather. A tiny log hut near Father Brown's lodge serves as a first-aid station. Father Brown has the key and only opens the first-aid station on the rare occasion when someone specifically requires medical attention.

I am surprised to meet a young Inuit woman at Father Brown's cabin – Margaret Steen. She seems to be about my age and is frying meat on a wood stove when we enter the brightly painted kitchen of the missionary's home. The slender, long-haired young woman looks up at me silently and returns to cooking. Her response to my friendly greeting is merely a nod. A woman in the priest's house? My misgivings are now on full alert.

As we sit down to dinner of caribou steaks on our first night together, surprise turns to dismay when I learn that

Father Brown is no longer conducting his duties as a priest; instead, he is running the Colville Lake Fishing Lodge for wealthy American tourists. Margaret, who is from Tuktoyaktuk[9], helps him manage the resort. Father Brown plans to marry Margaret as soon as he gets his dispensation from the Vatican, which I later learn is in the mail sack that he picked up today in Norman Wells.

The news hits me hard as the realization dawns on me – my mission to work with the First People of Canada is doomed. Instead of serving the natives, I am to work for Father Brown as he hosts rich visitors at his private fishing lodge. What on earth have I gotten myself into? I did not come to this native community to be a housekeeper, but it seems that will be my lot in life for the foreseeable future. Confused and torn, I say good night to Father Brown and Margaret and find my way to a bunk bed in one of the guest cabins, where heavy curtains darken the sun's unrelenting rays. There, I lie awake for hours, feeling disoriented and wondering what in heaven's name I can possibly contribute to the Dene people who live in this secluded setting.

My situation is precarious. I am totally dependent on Father Brown's hospitality and will have to do my best to maintain a positive relationship with him while building connections with the native people during my free time. I had hoped to spend my days getting to know the Dene, learning their language and customs, and offering my services as needed to help them with their daily tasks. Instead, I will be a chambermaid and waitress at a fishing lodge – not exactly what I had in mind when I set off on this journey five days ago.

Alone in the dark room late at night, I listen for the sound of a train. Trains had been a constant in my life. Growing up in Edmonton, I was accustomed to the nightly rumble of locomotives in the distance, usually accompanied by a far-off whistle. That comforting sound had lulled me to sleep for my

---

[9] Located farther north, close to the Arctic Ocean.

entire life. But there are no trains north of the Arctic Circle. How silly of me. Instead of a train, I hear birds chirping and children calling. Constant sunlight changes the rhythm of daily life. I'm in a different world or maybe a different universe.

I pray for guidance, asking God to provide me with some direction. Finally, I drift off into a light sleep until a thunderstorm awakens me. The pitter-patter of raindrops on the cabin roof is somehow soothing. I listen to the rain for a few minutes, then roll over and go back to sleep.

Morning dawns cool and damp. The world is fresh again, restored by the healing rain. A thick morning layer of cloud gives way to intense sun. I've arrived at my destination and am determined to make the best of it. Over breakfast, however, my hopes are dashed again. Despite my attempts to make conversation, Margaret remains silent and withdrawn. Then Father Brown coldly outlines my responsibilities. In exchange for room and board, I am to cook and clean for the guests who are scheduled to arrive in the coming days. The list of my responsibilities includes outdoor assignments such as yard work and washing the airplane as well as indoor tasks such as making beds and washing laundry by hand.

"But how will I get to know the people?" I ask, aghast.

"When your chores are done, you can do whatever you want," is the curt reply.

Fine. I start immediately on my first task – cleaning the guest cabins. Without running water or electricity, my options are limited. A broom, a bucket of soapy water, rag and scrub brush will have to suffice. Father Brown is not satisfied until the rooms are spotless. Then it's on to the next chore – sweeping dust and cobwebs from the verandah of each cabin. Then cutting back the bushes around the cabins. Then chopping wood for the wood stove and hauling water from a hole chopped in the ice covering the pristine lake.

The lake is still completely frozen over, but the ice is already beginning to recede around the shore. And the sun is scorching. Although it is only May, the thermometer in full sun on Father Brown's front porch reads 94° Fahrenheit (34° Celsius). No wonder I am sweltering. By noon, I feel as if I've done a full day's work.

We sit down to lunch of fried fish with bread and beans. Our diet over the coming weeks primarily consists of fish from the lake, caribou or moose meat, oatmeal porridge, canned goods and home-made bread or bannock (a quick bread made without yeast and usually fried). I've been up North for less than a week and already I miss milk, eggs, fresh fruit and vegetables.

After lunch, my overseer grants me a short reprieve, and I am off like a shot to get to know my neighbours. I walk past the breathtakingly beautiful Our Lady of the Snows chapel that now stands idle. To reach the homes of the Hareskin Dene people, I follow a narrow dirt path over the rough terrain, skirting mud puddles and willow thickets. A mouse scurries across the path. Snowbirds flutter in the bushes and on the ground nearby. I swat away swarms of gnats. Up ahead is a scene of mild chaos. Women and men working outdoors, snarling dogs, open fires, toddlers with bare bums … so much is happening in the little community.

I edge sideways past a line of hungry sled dogs chained to posts in the ground. The eight animals seem wild. Pure muscle and weighing almost as much as I do, they lunge against their chains, snapping and growling at me. Are the creatures part wolf? How can the owners possibly train these ferocious beasts to pull a sled? If the chains break, I am dead! I keep a fearful distance, giving the huskies ample room as I pass by.

I count 14 log houses and 6 tents, with about 25 adult residents and an unknown number of babies, toddlers and small children. Dogs outnumber people by a long shot. Looks like there are at least 7 - 9 sled dogs for every family unit, each sinewy animal with a voracious appetite. Must take a lot of fish to keep them fed. Some of the cabins are empty because people come and go from the tiny settlement at will, spending weeks at a time out in the bush. Living off the land is second nature to these strongly independent people. Joel and Susan have set up house in a one-room cabin where they will spend their month of research.

Everyone I see is busy, busy, busy. What appeared at a distance to be chaos is actually an orderly sequence of activities. Women tend fires under large pots where caribou hides are being boiled with brains to soften the skins for tanning. Phew! The stench makes me gag. Little boys use sharp knives to carve wood or caribou antlers into implements and miniature figures. Men are out on the frozen lake with their dog teams. Through holes carved in the ice, they check their gill nets for fish. Other men are on shore, mending nets and feeding fish to the dog teams. Teenagers haul water from holes chopped in the lake, carrying the buckets back to their tents. Everyone looks at me and grins timidly when I meet their eyes. Many beckon me over with a friendly gesture. I ask a question in English and get a response in their language. Then we just laugh together.

I wander among the Dene people smiling and waving, grateful for their presence. I realize that I have been flung into an environment vastly different from anything I have ever known – a new world of foreign sights, smells and sounds. The air is fragrant with wood smoke and dry pine needles. Swarms of black flies, mosquitoes and other nameless insects buzz around me. Beaver skins are stretched between poles to dry. Little old ladies sit in the sun smoking their pipes. Women are stirring big pots of steaming liquid over open fires. Ravens with glossy black wings perch on tent poles and peer at me quizzically. Their raucous calls are not unpleasant.

Even the sun shines in a different way. In the light of the late evening sun, the tiniest pebble casts a long shadow. Slanting golden rays imbue the entire landscape with a shimmering incandescence.

When I look around Colville Lake, I know there are things that I am not seeing. I am sensing the Dene world through the eyes of an outsider, a non-Dene person. Invisible elements are at work here in this community. I can't begin to understand their language, their culture, their history, their family life or their complicated genealogy. As I get to know the people, their extensive kinship ties confuse me. Affiliations are complicated due to informal adoptions and often different last names within the same family. But I feel oddly at home and welcome in the midst of the companionable hubbub that is our shared bush camp.

The ice on the lake thins visibly every day, receding further from the shoreline almost before my very eyes. More and more open water appears until one day I realize the ice is completely gone. Within eight weeks, the ice will begin to reappear – first as a morning skiff of frost, then accumulating daily until the dense winter ice measures more than six feet thick and is strong enough to support many tons of heavy equipment and machinery.

With the ice now off the lake, the men immediately set their nets in the open water. They need a constant supply of fish to feed their families and their ravenous dog teams. The women will preserve the fish by slicing it thinly and hanging it to dry in the unending sunshine or over hot coals.

Father Brown flies to Inuvik to exchange the Cessna's wheels for floats so that he can land at his own dock in front of the fishing lodge. I am tasked with cleaning and waxing the exterior of the Cessna (call letters CF-SLA, affectionately known as SLA). One memorable day I am standing on the floats, reaching overhead to scrub the wings of the plane, when I lose my balance and end up in the freezing water of Colville Lake. I scramble out quickly and shiver on the dock, gasping and laughing ruefully while my Dene friends chuckle at my predicament. Just a week ago, while there was still ice on the lake, some of the Dene kids had gone swimming. They broke off chunks of ice and gave them to me, giggling, as I stood safely on the warm dock. Now that I have tested the polar water myself, I have a new respect for the children's ability to withstand the frigid temperature.

And so the days and weeks pass … Father Brown, now to be known as Bern Will Brown, teaches me how to filet a fish and instructs me in unique aspects of the northern environment. Showing me a thin, stunted spruce tree, he explains that the little specimen took more than a hundred years to grow in the harsh Arctic climate. He describes the many practical uses for *babiche*, which is rawhide or sinew formed into long, thin strips. Babiche is strong and has multiple uses; the sinew is especially effective for making snowshoes and for stringing the back or seat of a chair.

During the hot summer months, Father Brown keeps caribou meat frozen in his below-ground permafrost 'freezer' that he has carved into a natural hummock on the lakeshore beside his house. Permanently frozen ground lies a few inches below the thin soil cover in the Arctic, and the man's natural freezer is a source of wonder to me. Father Brown is highly inventive, making use of available resources in innovative ways. Tales of his life in the North are riveting. My boss regales me with stories about various guests he has hosted at the Colville Lake Fishing Lodge. All visitors to Colville Lake have journeyed long distances to get there, and some – like the archbishop who came from Rome to bless Our Lady of the Snows church in 1964 – have made an extraordinary trek from afar.

Lacking a camera to record the unique beauty of my surroundings, I want to keep a diary. Father Brown finds an old notebook that had been left behind by an American anthropologist last summer. Thank you! Now I can record some of my thoughts and observations. Stretching out on the dock under the glare of the midnight sun, I begin writing in the thin coiled scribbler. I also write letters home to my family in Edmonton, begging all the pilots who happen to pass through our region to please mail the letters when they get to Yellowknife.

One sunlit afternoon, Father Brown, Margaret and I take his big boat, The Loon, (*Quimpa* in the Dene language) to his cabin at the north end of the lake, where I catch, clean and filet the fish for our dinner while he and Margaret maintain the outpost buildings. By now, gutting fish and building a fire is second nature to me. Eating fresh trout fried over an open flame makes the effort well worthwhile. We return to the main lodge late that night, the sun still bright in the sky.

Every day is a new learning experience with this strong-willed entrepreneur. Still, it bothers me that I am serving him instead of the Dene people, and Father Brown's nightly diatribes against the Indians are beginning to rankle. I don't like him criticizing my new friends. I want to believe the best about people. Besides, nobody's perfect. Only two years ago, Father Brown sat in our Edmonton living room and spoke about the native people in glowing terms. What made him change so dramatically? Best for me to remain silent and avoid antagonizing my employer.

Two weeks into my stay, I decide it's time to have a bath. After hauling four buckets of water from the lake, I heat the water on the wood stove, then pour it into the only bathtub in town. Sinking into the warm water feels like pure luxury. For 15 minutes, I revel in the rare comfort of soaking my body. But it's hard to get the temperature just right and the water cools off quickly. When I stand up to dry off, the grey bath water is grimy from the dust and dirt that has accumulated on my body. Now I have to empty the bathtub and scrub the soap residue from the sides and bottom of the tub. It has taken me all afternoon to have a bath and I am still not exactly squeaky clean. No wonder the scent of body odour is pervasive in our little bush camp.

The roar of an aircraft every few days alerts us when outsiders approach. Guests arrive by helicopter, Twin Otter, de Havilland Beaver, Cessna, DC-3, Argus and Norseman. Margaret and I serve lunch to geologists, fishermen, miners, game wardens and government workers who sit on the verandah, overlooking the lake and talking with Father Brown. Imperial Oil staff pay us a visit. A helicopter pilot from

Okanagan Helicopters flies me to Fort Good Hope just to witness my delight in flying low over the spectacular scenery. This community on the banks of the Mackenzie River is known to the Dene as *Radelie Ko* (where the rapids are). Mining exploration company representatives drop in for coffee and pie. Kenaston Drilling arrives unannounced. Even the Royal Canadian Air Force flies in for an afternoon, just stopping by to say hello because they were in the general vicinity. The Shell Oil plane lands at our dock with my cousin as pilot – what a surprise! Chatting with Bevan revives my spirits. Reminders of home are few and far between.

Father Brown and a visitor discuss fishing tackle in a guest cabin with wolf skins on walls and floor.   NWT Archives © GNWT Dept of Info/G-1979-023-0234

Every few days, Father Brown flies to Norman Wells to pick up fishermen who will stay in the Colville Lake Fishing Lodge cabins. These visitors are affluent, middle-aged men who travel all the way from the United States of America to fish in the clear waters of Colville Lake, where they are guaranteed to land a whopper. Working alongside Margaret, I fry caribou steaks, brew coffee and bake apple pies for our hungry callers. To earn my keep, I also wash dishes, sweep the bunkhouses, make beds, dust furniture, organize the pantry and mop floors.

Father Brown's subjects for this northern Madonna and Child were Dene.

I also work outdoors. Every day my chores are different. I haul water from the lake, wash SLA, chop wood, varnish the log cabins, filet fish and run countless errands for the unrelenting Father Brown. Somehow, I can't find it in myself to call him anything but Father Brown despite his change in status. Force of habit, I guess. After more than twenty years of hard work in the North, Father Brown no longer feels an obligation to minister to the Indigenous population. He only wants to host affluent guests at his estate on the secluded lake. I guess my implacable taskmaster has earned the right to leave the priesthood, marry the woman he loves and run a resort for wealthy summer tourists.

4   Life in a Bush Camp

In 1971, Colville Lake was considered to be the most remote place in North America because it was only accessible by chartered aircraft. The little bush camp is not located on a water route, and overland travel on the tundra is extremely challenging, especially during the summer months when the terrain is spongy and uneven. Scheduled flights to the settlement began in 1986, when North-Wright Airways launched operations in the Sahtu. Unlike other communities that are located farther north, there are no government offices in Colville Lake. One of the last bush communities in the Northwest Territories, the hamlet is located 165 miles south of the Arctic Ocean and 31 miles north of the Arctic Circle.

*

The lake itself holds an allure that goes beyond its natural beauty. Under morning clouds, the waves are grey. After lunch, I marvel at a shimmering blue vista. Late at night, golden ripples flash in the bright evening sunlight. I fetch clear, cold water just off the dock and drink the refreshing liquid right from the lake. Walking back along the dock, I see willow bushes lining the lakeshore. A few stunted spruce trees grow in odd places. I step off the dock onto spongy tundra[10] and follow a meandering footpath where the patchy moss has worn down to dirt. Thousands of tiny, brilliant flowers grow directly out of the tundra, some strongly scented. Tufts of grasses spring up here and there, growing quickly with the constant sunlight. Lichen, the principal food of caribou, is abundant in the region around Colville Lake.

The Dene people have existed in harmony with the environment for thousands of years, finding subsistence from the land and water. One afternoon, I jump on to Jean-Marie's boat and we head across the lake to *Dugah* (White) Island to

---

[10] Small shrubs, grasses, mosses and lichens that can withstand Arctic weather conditions.

gather duck eggs with our friends. Jean-Marie teaches me how to test whether the egg is good to eat. If the egg sinks in water, it is fresh. If the egg floats, the chick inside is already maturing. Leave it alone! We gather 35 good eggs in just over an hour of wandering around the little island. I can't wait to fry them up and finally taste something different for dinner.

Dugah Island seems like a Martian landscape. The entire island is perfectly flat, with no vegetation growing more than three inches in height. The tundra here seems lifeless and inorganic, but I see small, bright flowers and berries nestled in the springy wasteland. Called 'cloud berries,' they are amber in colour and taste delicious. I step cautiously to avoid terns' eggs and caribou droppings.

Flying insects are impossible to escape during the Arctic summer. As the temperature climbs, mosquitoes, black flies, gnats and other winged creatures relentlessly seek any source of nourishment. I soon come to dread the whine of a single mosquito in my bedroom at night and the humming that accompanies a swarm of black flies gorging on a pile of fish guts. The people tell me that they have seen moose and caribou driven mad by bugs, plunging about wildly and diving into the lake to escape the vicious pests.

Father Brown and I wear mosquito nets to protect our heads from the swarms of pests, but the voracious insects can penetrate anything, biting through my denim jeans and crawling under the tiniest gap in my clothing. Bumps and welts all over my body keep me awake at night because I can't stop myself from scratching the itchy, swollen bug bites.

Tanning hides takes many days. I watch the Dene women boiling caribou hides with caribou brains, then stretching the hides over poles to dry in the sun. When I notice small holes in the hides, the Dene women explain the life cycle of the warble fly. Caribou are plagued by warble flies which lay their tiny eggs on the caribou skin. The eggs hatch into larvae which burrow beneath the hide, growing and moving under the caribou's skin. The adult flies finally emerge from the poor

44

animal, leaving a hole in the hide as they gnaw their way out of the tough skin. Must be terribly aggravating for the caribou – no wonder they seek relief in the lake.

Communication in the Arctic is complicated and challenging. Our choices are limited to written correspondence via the postal system and oral transmission via satellite radio. Mail delivery to Colville Lake is sporadic, unreliable and completely dependent on the good will of others. The mail is held at Norman Wells or Yellowknife until someone happens to fly in the vicinity of Colville Lake and agrees to drop off a mail bag, often weeks later.

This old medium-frequency radio set could receive and transmit on one channel (2240 KHz), making limited communication possible in the 1970s.

Although there are no telephones in Colville Lake, Father Brown has a headset connected to a satellite radio. Using his high-frequency radio set, he is able to contact other people who have similar equipment, including the air traffic control towers in other communities[11]. Everyone in the North listens to radio station CHAK for personal messages. People in various Arctic communities contact the radio station to broadcast messages to friends and relatives in other communities. I don't know the

_____

[11] Catholic priests had their own ground-to-ground channel.

names of the individuals, but I love hearing that "Myrtle in Aklavik is expecting a baby in August," or "Jack, please contact your parents so we know you are okay."

The weather is a serious topic of conversation every day because it can make the difference between life and death on land or water. The warm orange glow of the sun over the lake can be deceptive, lulling one into a false sense of security. Conditions above the Arctic Circle are apt to change suddenly and dramatically. Even during the brief summer, temperatures fluctuate wildly, from blistering hot to very cold within a few minutes. Sometimes blue sky is juxtaposed beside black clouds. And look out for those black clouds – torrential downpours leave huge mud puddles that quickly evaporate in the hot sun. The Dene tell me: "Weather is the boss." They accept all weather conditions without complaint. Blizzards and rainstorms provide an opportunity to hunker down with family and friends, reflect on life and tell stories. Sunny days are for hunting and fishing. In Colville Lake, the weather decides how we will spend our time.

I soon make friends with the few Dene who are fluent in English. Jean-Marie Oudzi and Alouie Codzi become my constant companions. As soon as the ice is off the lake, we go fishing together almost every day, catching four or five trout each within an hour. One sunny afternoon, I fight desperately to bring in a fish and am disappointed by its size when I finally land it in the boat. "Darn! I thought it was much bigger!" I exclaim in dismay. But my friends are laughing at me. "That's a good-sized Arctic grayling," they tell me. "It's close to five pounds and that's as big as they get."

Dark blue on the back and purple grey on the sides, the grayling has a beautiful dorsal fin and is unlike any fish I have ever seen. I filet the grayling when I get back to the lodge and fry it for dinner with Father Brown and Margaret. The flavourful meat is a pleasant-tasting surprise from our usual trout. In addition to trout, whitefish, pike, walleye, perch and grayling, we occasionally reel in a funny-looking fish that my

46

friends call a *loche*. The strange creature resembles a miniature sea monster.

One day I ask my friends about a haze of smoke in the distance. Alouie reminds me of the thunderstorm a few days ago. Lightning strikes have sparked wildfires nearby. This worries me, but my friend assures me that the fires will burn out before they reach Colville Lake. And he is right. Within a day or two, the smoke is gone and the air is clear again.

Most afternoons, I am free to wander through the settlement, making friends with old and young alike. The native part of the community is very different from Father Brown's enclave. Somehow, I feel as if I fit in among the canvas tents and rustic cabins. I am especially drawn to the beautiful, bronzed children who roam around together, older ones piggy-backing the toddlers.

When I was growing up, I loved caring for my siblings and babysitting children of all ages. Changing diapers and toilet training were second nature to me – I longed to be a mother with my own children someday. These Dene youngsters are particularly endearing, their sweet nature appealing to my maternal instincts. I play with them, hug them when they fall down, clean their scraped knees with lake water and wipe their runny noses with my sleeve. My heart is full when they look up at me with trusting brown eyes.

The boys and girls christen me *Sayday Marie*, which means 'younger sister Marie', because I am younger than their mother and auntie, Marie Kochon. These delightful children are curious about the light-skinned stranger in their midst; they watch me carefully as if memorizing every detail of my face and gestures. Crowding close to my side, the kids listen intently as I speak the foreign English language. I quickly learn the names of the little ones: Rolly, Sharon, Robert, Joseph, Curtis, Mark, Wilbert and many others.

The bright, inquisitive Dene children in Colville Lake learn quickly. Initially shy around me, they soon open up and actively participate in our outdoor games. Maybe I could teach these keen minds to speak English. But where to begin? Singing the *Alphabet Song* is completely meaningless to them. Never mind. Let's just play ball. Father Brown has provided a red rubber ball for our activities and we play 'keep away,' boys against the girls. Eagerly, the teams run after the ball, laughing and shouting. Even the toddlers are amused with our antics.

By now, at least ten or twelve children gather around me every day. We spend all of our time outdoors together, and we need a place to congregate and shelter from the sun. Fortunately, a teenager named Helen comes to my rescue. Helen is five years younger than I am. At fourteen years of age, this black-haired girl with almond eyes and a disarming smile is fluently bilingual. We communicate easily and she quickly becomes my closest friend. I am grateful when she translates my words so that the people of Colville will understand who I am and why I am here.

My young ally helps me pitch a makeshift tent that will keep the sun off and become a meeting place for me and the little ones. We choose a flat spot to erect our shelter and I dig into the tundra with a stick to find frozen ground! I hit permafrost within inches of the surface soil. Hard as concrete, the solid earth is impenetrable. Never mind. We can do this. Together, Helen and I chop skinny spruce tree saplings into poles. We tie the poles together to form an 'A' frame and beg a large piece of canvas from Helen's dad to drape over the posts. A sawed log serves as a table inside our makeshift 'school.'

The boys and girls cluster around me as I try to teach them how to say colours in English for our first 'lesson' under the canvas cover. I love their innocent little upturned faces and want only to make them happy. Maybe a sweet treat will motivate them to try to speak English. Disregarding the possible impact on the children's teeth, I snag a bag of coloured marshmallows from Father Brown's pantry for a simple lesson plan. I hold up each marshmallow individually and ask the kids to repeat the name of the colour after me. The marshmallow then becomes their reward for pronouncing the word correctly. The hungry children are eager for any kind of food and the goodies are *lakoh* (sweet).

Joel and Susan want to know what is going on inside our little shelter. The two Americans laugh merrily at the way I pronounce the word 'orange' so differently from their Bronx accent. Young Joseph cannot seem to wrap his lips around the vowel sounds, so little Sharon gets the orange marshmallow for best pronunciation. Even the big boys who usually hang around outside our tent are intrigued. Laughter and smiles on every face this afternoon.

My spirits are dashed when I return to the lodge for dinner. I should have asked Father Brown's permission to take those marshmallows from his pantry. He refers to my actions as 'theft.' Ouch! Truth be told, I am guilty as charged. In addition to today's marshmallows, I had snitched a cake mix last week. The children had been excited at the prospect of baking a lakoh cake using the only wood stove in town at Joe Martin's cabin. My little imps took turns stirring the cake mix. We laughed as we peeked in the oven and waited for our masterpiece to bake. Because the cake had no eggs, it fell apart and we ate the final product, a lakoh delicacy, by digging into it with spoons.

Now that I think about it … I have to admit that it was wrong of me to take the cake mix and marshmallows from Father Brown. Despite the kids' obvious enjoyment, I feel remorseful for taking Father Brown's treats without asking. Oh dear. I am not making a good impression with my boss. I am sorry that I stole goodies from his pantry to give to the Dene children, but deep down I also feel a bit rebellious. If only he would share with the people who live here … the people are hungry and Father Brown has ample provisions. It's just not fair. However, I don't want to wear out my welcome. Where would I go from here? I will just have to behave myself.

Visitors sat on the lodge verandah, overlooking the lake and talking with Father Brown.

In the days that follow, I continue to learn about my strange new environment on the edge of the Arctic Circle. The landscape that appeared so barren from the air is actually alive with small game and many species of waterfowl that feed on the enormous insect swarms. I am surprised that the wet muskeg is such a complex habitat. The Arctic ecosystem here in the bush camp is an intertwined matrix of plants, animals, land, water and humans.

Helen tells me that her Dene ancestors chose the site of Colville Lake because the location is known for its abundance of food, specifically caribou, fish and ptarmigan. The little settlement is located on the caribou migration route for good reason. The caribou herd is so vast that it takes more than two weeks for all the animals to pass by the Colville Lake homes twice a year. A Colville Lake hunter can stand in the doorway of his house and shoot a couple of caribou without disturbing the rest of the herd.

Fish are equally plentiful and are the major source of nourishment for dogs and humans. Loaded with protein, vitamins and minerals, fish from Colville Lake sustain life for the entire community. Everyone was hungry when I first arrived, but now that the ice is off the lake, Helen assures me that we will catch enough fish every day to satisfy the appetites of all the dogs and all the people.

This time of year also brings a never-ending supply of food in the form of geese, ducks, swans and ptarmigan. Ptarmigan are pure white, medium-sized gamebirds, similar to grouse or partridge, that range throughout northern Canada and Alaska. Colville Lake is called *Kah Bah Mi Tue* (ptarmigan net place) because it's easy to catch ptarmigan with old fish nets. Just hang the nets among the thick willows on the lakeshore. Ptarmigan nesting in the willow bushes are caught in the nets and make a tasty meal when cooked over an open fire or stewed in a pot.

So far, I have only spent a few dollars from my small supply of money. The cashless society in our tiny hamlet feels somehow freeing. The daily unit of measure is human, not monetary. We spend our days catching and preparing fish, playing with children, chatting and visiting. During the winter months, the men earn money trapping marten, mink, beaver, fox, wolves and wolverines, but for now everyone is blissfully free of financial concerns.

I have entered this Dene community through a door that opened into another world whose features I am only gradually beginning to discern, a way of life that is vastly different from anything I have ever experienced. Fragments of Dene life startle me, and I sense a profoundly different understanding of the world we inhabit, a throbbing pulse that is invisible to the eye. For example, they have an uncanny ability to evaluate someone intuitively, merely by observing that person's behaviour. Dene reality seems to be ordered in ways that I don't understand. Fascinated with the Dene world view, I want nothing more than to explore it fully. So I walk with them, laugh with them and listen to them.

Making friends is easy despite the language and culture barrier. Unlike the anthropologists, I am not studying the people. I just want to get to know them. Edward Oudzi, hammering shingles on a roof, is a few years older than me and much too busy to stop and talk. But the children are eager to spend time with the sociable white-skinned teenager in their midst. Since the adults are hard at work, I take responsibility for keeping the kids safely occupied and out of harm's way. With 24 hours of daylight, the rhythms of daily life are circular. It's almost impossible to keep track of time. Children play outdoors until well past midnight. They eat when they are hungry and sleep when they are tired.

I find it challenging to understand the thick accent when the people try to speak English, so I listen hard. Even more problematic for me is to repeat words in their language. I try to make sense of the unfamiliar sounds and confusing tones of the Dene speech. When I attempt to pronounce a word, everyone laughs gleefully. I can tell these delightful people are teasing me, but I don't know what they are saying. (Later, I learn that the boys taught me to say vulgar words in their language.)

The Dene voice compels me to listen closely. Speech cadence and inflections are vastly different from those of a native English speaker. Some of the vowels are lengthened (eg., Reeeeeeeeally? Hooooooonestly!) and other words are shortened so that I can hardly tell the difference between 'yuh' for 'yes,' and 'nuh' for 'no.' Grammatical constructions are different, too. Dene speakers will often begin a sentence with the object, then switch to the subject. For example, someone might say, "Him, he is a good hunter." Or "Her, she knows how to bead." Does this manner of speaking reflect the grammar of the Dene language?

The timing between words and sentences is also different. Most notable are the long pauses. I need to be patient and wait my turn to speak. Otherwise, it seems like I am interrupting their train of thought. When I ask a question, I have to wait a long time for the answer. Maybe they are translating twice in their minds – first understanding my question, then formulating their answer, and finally translating their response. These long silences remind me to think before I speak.

The people of Colville Lake don't often ask questions. Instead, they will make an observation that I can then accept or question. Sometimes they will make a statement with an upward inflection at the end to indicate that it is actually a question. They accept things that happen – good or bad – without passing judgment and without dwelling on it. There seems to be no Dene word to express *hello, goodbye, he* or *she*. No gender distinction when referring to a person. Because their language does not distinguish male from female pronouns, this might be the reason that the Dene frequently mix up *he* and *she* when speaking English.

I don't realize until much later how much I am learning just by being with the Dene. Especially in the older folks, I am beginning to see the dignity inherent in the Dene nature, as well as their leadership qualities, strength and resilience. I am astonished when Johnny and Madeline Blancho return to Colville Lake with their infant son after spending two months camping in the bush. No one thinks it is unusual to camp outdoors for months at a time with a newborn, depending only on your wits for survival.

The older Dene love to tell stories and readily share their opinions with me. But when the Dene have nothing to say, they say nothing at all. Even their silent communication is instructive. No need for idle chitchat. We are content to sit together in companionable silence. Old and young alike are highly observant, always watching quietly and rarely showing emotion.

A strong sense of responsibility to friends and family permeates the Dene lives. They share fish, bannock and caribou meat freely with each other. Confrontation is avoided.

People who disagree with each other stay away from each other without airing their grievances.

The Dene are highly spiritual. Christianity is closely aligned with their traditional teachings, and the people of Colville Lake have embraced Catholicism. Saying grace before meals, thanking the Creator, praying the rosary every evening and asking God for guidance all seem to come naturally to young and old. Sadly, because Father Brown is no longer conducting the duties of a priest, the log church stands idle except when young and old congregate for Sunday rosary. I am disappointed that the former priest no longer associates with these extraordinary people, but I won't let him discourage me from befriending them.

It seems that the Dene don't like to say 'no.' My suggestions – to play ball or learn English or go fishing – are invariably welcomed. Even if they don't know how to do something, they will give it a try. Night and day, everyone is industrious, busily occupied with cleaning hides, repairing nets, carving, sewing, cooking, tending fires, gathering moss and other camp chores.

Tagging along behind me, the children try to repeat the strange foreign sounds they hear me making. Even the youngest children quickly learn to say, "Let's do it!" and "Let's play ball!" in English. With their swift and spontaneous actions, the youngsters sure keep me on my toes.

The older boys are macho, play-fighting and loudly bossing each other around. Maybe they are showing off to impress me? On the other hand, the girls rarely speak up and don't display emotion. Their dark eyes watch my every move. I want to make friends with Sarah, but she averts her eyes bashfully and seems to have nothing to say to me.

One day, I am sitting in our tent with the little kids crowded around me. They are learning to sing "O Canada," though I don't think the words mean anything to them. Suddenly we hear a loud commotion. Dogs are barking and howling. Someone is yelling. What's going on? We rush out of the tent to see a funny sight. Jean-Marie has hitched up his dog team to a sled. The huskies have been chained up with no exercise for more than a month and now they are running wild. We are just in time to see Jean-Marie tumble off the dogsled into the willow bushes. The dogs are hopelessly tangled in their harnesses. Jean-Marie jumps up, unscathed, and attempts to bring order to the chaos. The kids are giggling, and I join in their glee. No one is hurt and the lively scene makes us all laugh.

Everyone in Colville Lake shares their homes freely, even with strangers. Aside from Father Brown's buildings, there are no locks on the cabin doors. The tents are particularly vulnerable, but no one seems to worry about theft. There is little privacy and very few secrets in our tiny community. As I walk along the dirt path one day, an elderly granny smoking a pipe motions for me to come inside her canvas tent home. Pulling aside the tent flap, I step on to a plywood platform and enter a very pleasant living arrangement. The wood stove holds a dented, blackened kettle. A grimy stovepipe pokes up through the tent cover that forms the roof. Religious pictures and icons grace the canvas walls. Dried fish hangs on a skinned log above the stove. Blankets in disarray cover a mattress on the floor. This is a cozy and comfortable living area, suffused with sunlight filtered through the canvas ceiling.

Laughing, my grey-haired hostess chatters away in her own language. I have no idea what she is saying but I grin happily. I agree that it's pretty funny for a white teenager to be a guest in her home. "Wineta," she says with a smile, gesturing toward one of two rickety chairs. I gather she wants me to sit down and stay a while; I'm more than happy to oblige. Picking up the battered tin kettle from the wood stove, the lady of the house pours tar-black tea into a chipped mug and passes it to me, all the while talking nonstop. I smile, nod and silently enjoy her companionship. She shows me where she is sewing beads in beautiful flower patterns on stroud, a wool duffel fabric. The thick cloth will form part of a knee-high winter moccasin for a family member. Clearly, this lovely lady is encouraging me to linger in her tent as long as I wish. It feels good to be accepted and welcomed into this close-knit Dene community.

Afternoons with the Dene people are fun filled. I jump in the boat with Alouie and Jean-Marie to check their gill nets for fish, play ball with the children and try my hand at stretching a beaver skin. With Helen as my interpreter, I am now able to converse with everyone in Colville Lake. That's when I learn that my initial instincts were correct – these good-natured people are, indeed, often laughing at me. In their own humorous way, the people of Colville Lake are constantly teasing each other. My arrival gives them the opportunity to poke fun at the strange white woman who is now living among them. I am tolerated with amusement in this friendly sanctuary. Life is good.

Dene men in Colville Lake are building a canoe in 1969, before I arrived.

Evening is visiting time. I play three-handed cribbage with Florence and George Barnaby on the plywood floor of their canvas tent. Their infant baby boy sleeps in a blanket suspended by strings from the rafters above us. Every once in a while, I hear the baby start to fuss. That's when I reach up to push the swing and gently rock him back to sleep.

After Florence skunks me at crib, I head over to another tent, where Alouie plays Dene love songs on his guitar. Brew pots are passed around from hand to hand. Men and women alike drink the contents, often to excess. Alcohol loosens inhibitions, and people who are ordinarily calm can erupt into a rage. Fistfights are not uncommon. One evening, I hold the hands of a sobbing young woman while Father Brown stitches up her scalp injury caused by an alcohol-fuelled quarrel. The next day, I swab the wound with disinfectant and smooth on ointment to prevent infection from setting in.

Many people keep a pot of home brew somewhere in their tent or cabin. Curious about the home-made alcohol, I sniff the contents of the tin basin and gag. What's in there? I am informed that raisins, water and yeast yield a potent beverage with high alcohol content. No raisins? Potato peels will do just fine. Leave the concoction to ferment for a few days, and the resulting beverage has the power to intoxicate those who imbibe. Not for me, thanks.

Everyone in Colville Lake loves to dance. Almost every night, someone plays a cassette tape or turns on a transistor radio to find a rock and roll station. The elderly sway to the music. Toddlers jump up and down. Old and young dance to the music of the Sixties, jigging[12] and partying until the wee hours.

Many adults in our bush camp like smoking or chewing tobacco and snuff (smokeless tobacco made from ground tobacco leaves). Women and men roll their own cigarettes. From a battered Player's tin, a person will pinch a few strands of tobacco between two fingers. Next, he pulls a thin piece of cigarette paper from a small cardboard pack and carefully rolls up the tobacco inside the paper. Moistening the paper with a

---

[12] Dancing characterized by rapid footwork.

bit of saliva on his tongue, he seals the edges. Now it's ready to smoke.

Other men tuck a bit of snuff or chewing tobacco into their cheeks, sucking on the shredded tobacco and spitting out a stream of brown saliva from time to time. Some men and women smoke tobacco in a home-made pipe made from a hollow goose bone, with a caribou vertebra serving as the bowl of the pipe.

Night or day, the sun barely moves above us. I can't tell how time is passing until I look at my watch. I need to get enough sleep that I can put in a solid day's work for Father Brown in the morning, so I am usually the first one to leave our evening get-togethers.

One afternoon, my three constant companions invite me to walk up to the cemetery together. I have never seen a more beautiful and peaceful environment. Scattered among the pine trees are five solitary graves, each surrounded by its own white and green picket fence. A crucifix on a stick, rosaries, wooden crosses, a drum – each grave is uniquely adorned with symbols from family members. Love is evident in the neatly tended plots. The silence is restorative. Even the ever-present bugs don't bother me in this secluded spot. Fascinated, I wander amid the graves, wishing I had a camera and trying to memorize every detail.

A few minutes later, I notice that my friends' behaviour is markedly different from mine. Yes, the cemetery is a lovely place, but their actions remind me that it is also sacred. Individually, each of my companions stops at the grave of a loved one, makes the sign of the cross and prays silently before moving on to the next fenced site. I immediately follow suit. Dropping to my knees beside a grave, I pray as best I can.

Heavenly Father, I am in a sacred place now, surrounded by the souls of the ancestors. Please guide me on this journey. I am grateful for this experience, but I don't know what I should be doing. Open my eyes. Show me how to serve the Dene. Please.

58

A strange sensation comes over me as I pray. My skin tingles and I can feel the spirits of the Dene ancestors surrounding me. An exquisite, over-all sense of harmony gladdens my heart. I want nothing more than to remain forever in this indescribable state of bliss. Time stands still. It seems a curtain has descended around my shoulders, filtering away the outside world. The minutes pass in a quiet reverie. Then, looking up, I see Jean-Marie, Helen and Alouie quietly waiting for me, ready to return to the village. We walk back down the hill together, each of us still lost in our own silent meditation.

Trees ring the cemetery in 2017, though no trees grew near Colville Lake in 1971. The tree line has moved north substantially in less than fifty years.

I know that Father Brown disapproves of me spending so much time with the natives. His snide remarks and nightly lectures about the "evil Indians" are wearing me down. For the past week, Father Brown has been especially brusque and withdrawn. It is evident that I have worn out my welcome in his resort. I have painted every room in every cabin, cleaned diligently and completed all the assigned tasks. Not much more I can do for him. My host has suggested more than once that it's time for me to leave, but I still have so much to learn about the Dene language and culture. Maybe it will take a lifetime.

The day after my cemetery visit, over dinner, Father Brown has news for me. Jack Wilder, general manager of Trophy Lodge on Great Bear Lake, has spent most of the day here in Colville Lake with Father Brown. I had served lunch to the friendly, outgoing man, then left him with Father Brown at the lodge while I played cards and went fishing with my friends. In my absence, the men had apparently discussed the 'Mary-Anne problem.' I am an unwelcome addition to Father Brown's life, and it seems he has now found a way for me to leave Colville Lake. Turns out that Jack needs another chambermaid at Trophy Lodge. Through Father Brown, Jack is offering me a job for the rest of the summer.

Taken aback, I ask, "What will I do at Trophy Lodge?"

"Same as you do here," replied Father Brown. "You will be a server and a chambermaid. That means you will clean rooms, serve guests, wash dishes, help the cook and make beds … you have experience and Jack is willing to pay you. The position includes free room and board at the resort. This way, you will earn enough money to pay your university tuition in September."

I can't argue with Father Brown's logic. My living arrangements in Colville Lake are dubious at best and fully dependent on Father Brown's magnanimity. His resentment towards my presence has been growing. It's not fair for me to impose on his goodwill any longer. Our relations are strained. Besides, the job is an opportunity to earn some badly-needed cash.

I had already decided to go back to university and earn a teaching degree. Educational credentials might enable me to come back to Colville Lake and teach the children something useful. I need to pay tuition fees and there is no way to earn money if I stay in that tiny hamlet. Maybe Trophy Lodge is the direction I need to go from here?

Contradictory feelings surge through me. I am falling in love with the Dene people here in Colville Lake. The kids run to greet me every day. How can I leave their smiling faces? I will miss my Dene friends terribly. But it's possible that a job at Trophy Lodge is the answer to yesterday's graveside prayer.

Over breakfast the following morning, Father Brown delivers his verdict. The unequivocal words leave no doubt. "You've been here for almost two months. It's time for you to leave. Jack will send a float plane for you tomorrow."

Tomorrow! Not enough time to say goodbye to each of the people who have filled my heart with such happiness. Not enough time to soak up the ambience – to breathe in the woodsmoke, listen to the ravens, taste the dry fish, feel the lake breeze on my face, play with the kids, laugh with the Elders and sip yet another cup of strong tea …

The thought of leaving behind these unique people saddens me immensely. I can't imagine what the future holds. I only know that I have been afforded a rare opportunity to live with men, women, babies, Elders, teens and children who are close to the land, who naturally live and breathe their deep Dene roots. I still have so much to learn about these remarkably resilient people. After two months, I am just beginning to make sense of their family connections, their ancient stories, their strengths and their spirituality.

Still, leaving Colville Lake is the only way for me to earn money and put myself through university. Armed with an education degree, I will be able to come back and truly make a difference in the lives of the remarkable people I have come to love as my own family. It is time to go, but what am I getting myself into at Trophy Lodge?

5   Trophy Lodge

*My destination, Trophy Lodge, is located on Great Bear Lake[13],
the largest lake entirely within the borders of Canada and the world's
eighth largest mass of cold fresh water. Four times the size of Prince
Edward Island, the lake's diverse ecoregions provide habitat for a
wide range of plants, animals and fish. Wildlife species include barren
ground caribou, moose, grizzly bear, muskoxen, fox, beaver, marten,
mink, muskrat, lynx, wolverine, Arctic hare, wolf and many others.
More than thirty different species of waterfowl are found on and
around this massive body of water. The only human habitation on
Great Bear Lake is the Dene community of Fort Franklin[14], nestled
on Keith Arm, near the outflow of the Great Bear River that flows
west, emptying into the Mackenzie River at Fort Norman.*

*

I leave my friends in Colville Lake slumped in the co-
pilot's seat of a little float plane, crying my eyes out all
the way to Trophy Lodge, 45 minutes southeast on
enormous Great Bear Lake. The people of Colville had become
like a family to me. They were so gentle, so funny, so wise in
the ways of the land. Despite the language and culture barriers,
old and young alike had accepted me with open arms and open
hearts.

I know that going to Trophy Lodge is for the best; still,
overwhelming grief rips through me when I climb aboard the
Beaver aircraft and look back at the tiny cluster of tents and
cabins for the last time. Tears trickle down my face and soak
my T-shirt. The pilot tries to make conversation with me but I
can't trust my voice. I just sob silently into my sleeve and stare
out the window of the plane at the barren tundra below.

---

[13] 31,000 km² (12,000 miles²), 446 m (1463 feet) deep

[14] Originally known as *Deline* (where the waters flow), the community
reverted to its Dene name in 1993.

Unbearable sadness grips my heart. Will I ever see my friends again?

When the limitless blue waters of Great Bear Lake come into sight, I begin to perk up. As far as the eye can see, the cobalt expanse glitters in the sunlight, punctuated with inlets, islands, and sheltered bays. Soon, log buildings appear in a clearing below us. Spruce trees, a board sidewalk and a path winding toward a clean sandy beach. Hmmmmmmmm …. This might not be so bad. I dry my tears, take a deep breath and steel myself. I can do this.

We land on the lake and taxi up to the float dock. Clambering down from the plane, I grab my suitcase and look around at my new surroundings. Trophy Lodge is situated in well-protected Ford Bay, on the Smith Arm of Great Bear Lake. From where I stand on the wooden float dock, I can see beyond the clear blue water and sandy beach to sturdy buildings. A woman is waving at me from the doorway of a building, so I walk towards her while the pilot secures the plane.

Rustic by most standards, the lodge I am approaching is palatial compared to my accommodation at Colville Lake. The main building at Trophy Lodge has a kitchen, dining room, lounge area and games room. Staff are housed in a series of small wooden cabins, with men's cabins separated from women's cabins by the main lodge. Guests stay in beautifully appointed bedrooms in another wing of the main lodge. A wooden boardwalk running over the boggy tundra connects all the buildings.

After my lengthy sojourn in Colville Lake, I am not prepared for first-rate accommodation, sandy beaches, electricity, a trained chef, indoor plumbing and, strangest of all, young men and women who, like me, are not native. They speak English without a trace of a Slavey accent.

Anglers are guaranteed to catch gigantic fish at Trophy Lodge.

I am the source of great curiosity among the staff of Trophy Lodge. So this is the girl who spent two months in the little bush community of Colville Lake. Aside from the occasional visitor, I hadn't spent any prolonged time with a white person other than Father Brown for almost eight weeks and I feel a bit awkward. Everyone seems to talk too fast and laugh too much. Fortunately, most of the fishing guides are Dene and I quickly gravitate to their companionship.

Lynn, manager of the female staff, greets me warmly and introduces me to the young women I will be working with over the next two months. Paulette, Marie, Cheryl, Susan, Karen and Kim are all University of Alberta students from Edmonton who are on their summer break. Like me, they have freckles and white skin. Unlike me their blouses are pressed, their hair is brushed and their smiles reveal perfect white teeth. I am painfully aware that my appearance is a striking contrast – dusty jeans, greasy hair and a strong scent of wood smoke. I smile tentatively at my new friends, wondering if I will ever feel comfortable with these delicate, dainty, feminine creatures.

Karen is a vivacious blonde with startling blue eyes who will be my roommate. It will be good to have a friend who is cheerful and fun-loving. Karen happily shows me to the little wooden cabin we will share. I detect an unfamiliar whiff of disinfectant. The shared bathroom actually has flush toilets – I'm impressed. I long to take a hot shower but will have to wait until later. Dropping my battered suitcase on the bunk bed next to hers, we return to the main lodge.

In the kitchen, I am astonished to see oranges, apples and tomatoes on the counter. The fridge even holds milk for my morning oatmeal. Fresh fruit and vegetables are flown into the resort every week as cargo in the baggage hold of the plane that brings the incoming guests. I am put to work immediately, chopping onions and running errands for Rosa, the cook. A commanding redhead with sharp facial features, Rosa runs an efficient operation by barking orders and brooking no nonsense from her underlings. We girls are on high alert whenever she speaks. An hour later, Cheryl tosses me an apron and tells me to start serving the guests their dinner. I quickly wash my hands, tuck my long hair behind my ears and put on a bright smile before walking into the dining room.

All twenty of our guests are middle aged men who love fishing. They have journeyed from across Canada and the United States, hoping to catch the biggest fish in the world here on ocean-sized Great Bear Lake. These wealthy tourists have paid top dollar to enjoy world-class fishing in a remote wilderness setting. The men cast their rods all week long to lure ancient lake trout that weigh fifty pounds or more. Some of the stunning specimens will be frozen whole. Then the carcass will accompany the guests back to their homes in the south, where the fish will be stuffed and mounted above a fireplace for display.

Fishermen prepare to board a Norseman float plane on Great Bear Lake in 1967.   NWT Archives © GNWT Dept of Info/G-1979-023-0292

My fellow lodge employees all work hard to ensure that every lodger has an experience he will remember forever.

Even before our guests finish eating dinner, the servers are already washing dishes and cleaning the kitchen. As the men leave the dining room, we are clearing tables and setting up for breakfast tomorrow morning. By 9:00 that night, I am emotionally and physically exhausted. Despite the sociable banter of the lodge staff, I am lonely for my Dene friends in Colville Lake. The children's faces swim before my eyes. Tears threaten when I least expect them. I'm ready for bed. The real workday begins tomorrow morning at 6:00 am and I need some sleep or at least some quiet time to myself.

"You can't go to your cabin," Karen giggles. "We're having a bonfire on the beach!"

Trophy Lodge is also above the Arctic Circle, where the sun never sets at this time of year; as soon as I am outdoors in the bright light, I begin to feel carefree again. A dirt path winds away from the main lodge, leading us to the lakeshore where a roaring fire is already burning. The sapphire blue lake stretches into the distance as far as the eye can see. Golden rays from the late-night sun imbue the scene with a surreal glow. The young men have placed logs around the fire for the girls to sit on. Someone strums his guitar and we all start singing *House of the Rising Sun*. Music, laughter, fire, sunshine, friendly companions … my spirits soar. This is going to be fun!

The next day, Karen lends me a T-shirt and jeans so that all my clothes can be laundered. Until I arrived at Trophy Lodge, I hadn't noticed the distinct odour that now permeates my clothing and body after seven weeks in the Colville Lake bush camp. My first shower in two months feels heavenly, and I am eternally grateful for hot running water.

The young women working as chamber maids and servers are friendly and exuberant; we all get along well. My roommate is especially likeable. Karen and I bond immediately. Turns out that Karen's family home is not far from mine. Though we attended different schools, we were both baptized at Saint John the Baptist Roman Catholic Church in Edmonton. We share the same zany sense of humour and dissolve into laughter at the slightest provocation.

Some of the young men are also university students from Edmonton but most are Dene from Fort Franklin. The young men work as fishing guides for Trophy Lodge. Each guide is assigned one or two guest fishermen. For almost a full week, the guides spend every day with their guests on the boats. The guide escorts his angler by boat to the best fishing spots on the lake, cooks a 'shore lunch' at noon, provides information about the lake and generally acts as a friendly, knowledgeable companion. The shore lunch consists primarily of freshly caught fish, fileted and fried over an open fire with potatoes and onions. Sandwiches, cookies and apples complete the menu if the men are still hungry. Guides eat lunch with their guests, sitting on large flat rocks or a pebble beach on the peaceful shores of Great Bear Lake.

I long for the children and my friends in Colville Lake, so I look to the Dene guides for the comfortable companionship that I am missing. During our first night around the bonfire at Trophy Lodge, I quickly make friends with a homely 26-year-old Dene named John. In John I find a kindred spirit. Plain-spoken and somewhat rough around the edges, my new-found companion was born on the land and can read it like a book. He seems unconsciously attuned to the natural environment. Every bush, stream, animal track and bird has a story behind it, and the down-to-earth young man is happy to share his traditional knowledge with me. John's understanding of his environment is fascinating, and I love exploring the unusual terrain with him.

Every day I finish my chores as quickly as possible so that John and I can go tramping through the bush together. I am a traveller in a foreign land, and John reads the signposts for me. One afternoon, John shows me a bush where a grizzly bear had feasted on berries. With guidance from my Dene companion, I can make out faint claw marks in the tundra. My new-found friend warns me about bears, explaining how to protect myself from predators in the wild.

Later that day, I laugh when John points out a killdeer running along the sand in front of us, pretending to have a broken wing by fluttering its wing on the ground. This graceful plover lays its eggs in a shallow depression scratched into the bare ground. Wide open and exposed, the nest is not the safest place for her eggs, so the killdeer is trying to distract us and lure us away from its nest. Its actions have the opposite effect on me. I quickly spy the well-camouflaged nest with its three speckled eggs, but we leave it alone. John explains that the eggs are good eating, in the event that I am ever lost in the wilderness without food. My Dene friend is teaching me survival skills. I tell John the lesson about testing eggs that I had learned on Dugah Island with my Colville Lake friends. John says that some of the people from Colville Lake are originally from Fort Franklin. He knows my friends – what a coincidence!

The killdeer is only one among thousands of waterfowl winging overhead, bobbing on Great Bear Lake and fluttering on shore. John identifies Arctic terns, geese, ducks and others that he can only name in the Dene language. Though the Arctic is a hostile environment from October through May, the entire ecosystem changes dramatically during the brief northern summer. Twenty-four hours of daylight and an abundance of food provide favourable breeding conditions for millions of migrating birds. Some fly all the way from Mexico to the Arctic Circle and then back again within the space of a few short months.

Despite being frozen over for almost ten months of the year, the fresh water of Great Bear Lake teems with trout, Arctic char, grayling, whitefish, herring, loche and northern pike. The largest freshwater fish on the planet are found in this vast inland sea. John tells me that the trout in Great Bear Lake are huge because they can live for a hundred years or more. During the winter months, some fish remain active. Others hibernate well below the ice in the deepest parts of the lake. As soon as the ice begins to melt in April, the fish wake from their slumber and start feeding. During the long hours of sunlight from May until September, the trout grow rapidly and will bite at anything that comes near them. They are plentiful and easy to hook, so fishermen at Great Bear Lake are guaranteed to catch all the fish they want. The fish are cleaned and flash frozen when the boats return to the lodge. Each guest's fish is identified, then packed in insulated tubs for the long journey back to the United States, where the angler's friends and family will enjoy a few meals of sumptuous trout or grayling from the bounty of Great Bear Lake.

The lodge guests compete to catch the biggest trout every day; the friendly competition takes place on the dock when the boats return from their day on the lake. Each large fish is hooked by the gills to a scale; the weight is duly recorded to cheers and applause from the guides and fellow fishermen. One day, I am near the dock when an American angler is weighing his 53-pound fish, the heaviest so far this summer. Our guest wants me to be in the picture, so I dutifully step up beside the trout and smile for the camera. After the shutter clicks, I look down into the mouth of the man's enormous trout, only to see … sticking up from the gaping maw … three or four small fish tails.

"Look at all the little fishies!" I laugh. But the American fisherman is not amused. He glares at me. What have I done wrong? Quickly, the man's guide interrupts. "Well, of course, that big trout was feeding when we caught him. So he swallowed the hook at the same time that he was eating the little fish." Oh, that explains it. Still, I can't help wondering why his guest is so mad at me. I guess some things are better left unsaid. (Later, I learn that some of the more competitive anglers stuff smaller fish down the throat of the big fish to increase the weight.)

For the next six weeks, I work as a server and chambermaid at Trophy Lodge on Great Bear Lake. I make beds, do laundry, peel onions, wash dishes, clean windows, scrub bathrooms, serve breakfast and dinner … for ten to twelve hours a day, all of us work REALLY hard. We play hard, too. Sitting around the beach fire chatting and singing under the light of the midnight sun, sand between my toes, laughter on my lips and music in my ears, I couldn't be happier. My fellow employees are creative, smart and funny.

The people in Colville Lake are known as Hareskin Indians, and some of the people in Fort Franklin are known as Dogribs. It's somewhat confusing, but I learn that they all consider themselves to be Dene, sharing similar ancestry and lifestyle. The language spoken by the Dene guides sounds like what is spoken in Colville Lake, though the young men chuckle at my pronunciation. My new Dene friends also joke about the bad words my Colville Lake friends taught me to say in Slavey. We seem to be always laughing together. I feel more comfortable with the natives than I do with the white employees, so I sit with the guides at the Dene table during our nightly staff dinners. I notice that the tables appear to be segregated. Curiously, I am the only white person who sits with the Dene guides.

I am surprised that the non-Dene keep to themselves when we can learn so much from our native friends. The language itself is fascinating because the sounds and syntax are entirely different from English. Our Dene companions can explain unique features of the Arctic environment. And they are endlessly entertaining. The Dene deftly perform rope tricks and sleight-of-hand with cards. They tell funny jokes. These young men are never arrogant, as some of the white guides tend to be. So why am I the only white person who appreciates them? I dismiss my uneasiness as needless worry. Still, I'm not sure where I fit in here at Trophy Lodge. I often feel like I am the odd one out. I didn't question my place at Colville Lake – being with the natives felt perfectly natural. But not here, with so many white people around and a hierarchy of responsibilities.

One memorable day, I jump on the float plane that is going to Fort Franklin for fuel. Walking down the main street of the tiny community with one of the Dene guides, I feel strangely at home. As George points out the church and dock in his hometown, I listen carefully but my mind is elsewhere. Fort Franklin somehow feels like a sacred place. The feeling reminds me of the Colville Lake cemetery. A phenomenon even greater than the vast blue water of Great Bear Lake is calling me. Maybe things that are invisible to the eye can be sensed in other ways? For some reason, I want nothing more than to make this special location my home. Our visit to Fort Franklin is all too short and soon we are scrambling back into the plane again, returning to our temporary home at Trophy Lodge. The mysterious sensation subsides as we get farther away from Fort Franklin, but a kind of residual spiritual awareness lingers within me for hours.

The days pass quickly until the moment that turns my life upside down once again. I am with the other servers at the counter in the kitchen making sandwiches to pack in the shore lunches when two Dene boys arrive at the kitchen door. We had heard a float plane land at the dock half an hour earlier and wondered who might be arriving at our resort in the middle of the week.

Framed in the entrance to the kitchen, both young Dene men seem awkward and shy. One of the boys doesn't look up at all. Both are named Travis, and the one who won't look up is the most incredibly attractive young man I have ever laid my eyes on. Thick, wavy black hair. Wiry body. Dark brown eyes. Red bandanna knotted around his forehead. Buckskin vest decorated with beaded floral designs. Broad shoulders tapering to a narrow waist. About six feet tall, the man's skin is the perfect suntan shade that I have tried in vain to achieve on my own skin, using iodine and baby oil. What a dreamboat!

My heart quickens and I feel the blood rush to my cheeks. I instantly look down again and go back to buttering bread while Karen talks with the boys. The young men have just arrived on the float plane from Fort Franklin and they will be working for Trophy Lodge as fishing guides. The boys are hungry, so Rosa fries up bacon and eggs for a quick lunch.

I can't stop myself from glancing again at the tall, handsome one – high cheekbones, strong jawline and a surprisingly wide grin that reveals even white teeth. Just a glimpse of his profile makes my heart skip a beat. But neither of the quiet, unassuming young men notices me. Both boys eat quickly with their eyes cast down, murmur their thanks and leave without looking at any of us girls.

When I finish work that night, I go looking for John and find him walking down by the lakeshore. I run over to my friend. "John," I pant. "Who are those two guys that arrived today?"

"Oh! That's my brother and my cousin," he laughs. "Don needs a couple more guides, so I recommended these boys. They will start guiding tomorrow."

"Which one is your brother?" I want to know. "Travis," he replies. "But they are both named Travis!" I exclaim. John seems amused. "Well, you'll find out soon enough."

I don't have to wait long to discover that John's brother is the man of my dreams. Within minutes, I see the good-looking Travis walking towards us. As he steps over a fallen log, my dreamboat grins at his brother and calls out, "Who's your friend, John?"

I laugh and try to catch the young man's eye. Travis turns to his brother with a shrug but before he does, I see a smile playing around his lips. That's how we met. The three of us quickly become fast friends and spend all our free time together, tramping through the woods whenever we can get away from the lodge.

Later that night, when the guides and waitresses are all relaxing in the staff lounge, Travis picks up his guitar. He is a musician, too! The perfect combination of everything desirable in a man. Travis' hands seem sculpted. I can't take my eyes off his strong, perfectly formed fingers softly picking out the melodies. Travis and I stay up until 4 am that first night, just talking and talking. He is smart and gentle and sweet, with fascinating stories of Dene life. I can't quell the romantic feelings welling up inside me.

As the days pass, I see Travis' character revealed in words and actions. His devotion to his family, especially to his older brother, is endearing. Respect for Elders is evident in the stories he tells me about his parents and grandparents. I admire his gentle way of discussing negative situations without anger or resentment. He has long-standing friendships with people he has known his entire life. Talking with this fascinating Dene man fills me with hope and excitement.

Karen is the only one who is in on my secret. I don't dare tell anyone else about my romantic feelings for fear of the gossip that will spread like wildfire. The first few times I am with Travis, I feel an initial blaze of colour in my cheeks, but he is so easy to talk to that very quickly I am myself again. With so many people around us at all times, I have to hide my raw feelings and carry on with easy banter. The young man's calm, self-assured presence never fails to put me at ease. Very soon, Travis and I are spending every possible minute together.

6   My Dene Boyfriend

Travis was born less than a year before me in a fish camp near Tulit'a, close to the Mackenzie River. He says, "I am the land. The land is me. My bones are the same as the mountains. My blood is like the rivers. My skin is like the dirt covering the earth. Anything that harms the land also harms me." Later, when we are talking about Great Bear Lake, Travis tells me, "All I know for sure is the lake is the boss. When I am out on the lake, I can only do what the lake allows me to do."

The day I began my journey to the north in 1971 was the same day that Travis turned twenty years old. As I was scrambling into the cockpit of a little airplane in Edmonton, he was out on the land, hunting caribou with his dad. My Dene boyfriend is eager to learn about everything, including life south of the Arctic Circle. His questions to me are thought-provoking. I'm learning from him, too. Travis thinks about the environment around us in a different way than I do. His deep relationship with the natural world unveils a perspective that my teenaged mind had never dreamed of.

"We are a small part of nature. The land, the lake, the caribou … they do not belong to us any more than the sunlight, the wind and the shadows belong to us." I nod in agreement. "Even when I am by myself on the land, I am not alone. The earth is my teacher. The trees, the wind and the animals are my relatives, and they are always talking to me. We understand each other." I can feel my mind-set shifting, reorienting to the Dene world view.

Travis tells me that his homeland is known as *Denendeh*, Land of the People. I notice that the word for his land actually contains the word for people (Dene), further reinforcing the interconnectedness of the land and the people.

"Mother Earth has blessed us with all we need. I was born in the wilderness and the moss was my diaper. The water cleanses me and heals me, the land gives me food and shelter, the plants give me medicine and clean air to breathe. The animals even give us our music because we make drums from caribou hide." Travis laughs and looks at me. "I love making you understand why it is so important to protect Mother Earth because there is no other world like this one ... unless you want to go to Pluto ... hahahaha!"

Serious again, he says, "We are only passing through this life, and we need to leave the world a better place for our children and grandchildren." I am surprised that a twenty-year-old man is already thinking about the generations to come.

I can tell that Travis has been thinking about how he can explain to me the strength of his connection with the land because the next day he tells me, "I heard a quote from John F. Kennedy, and I changed it around: 'Ask not what the land can do for you; ask what you can do for the land.'"

Travis' reference to JFK sparked a conversation about the ongoing unrest in the United States under the Nixon administration. Bloody race riots and the slaughter of American soldiers in the Vietnam war horrified all Canadians. I had met a few draft dodgers in Edmonton over the past few years. These were young men who had fled to Canada to avoid conscription in the U.S. military. My dad referred to them as 'conscientious objectors.' Lacking access to newspapers or magazines in far-off Fort Franklin, Travis knew very little about the turmoil in the USA.

When I stopped talking, Travis seemed pensive. My companion was quiet for a few minutes, deep in thought. Then he spoke up.

"The Elders told us how to handle a dog team. When the team is not getting along, you can't change the whole team. Just change the leader. The others will fall into line. Then you'll be okay."

Seems like the perfect metaphor for the political situation I had just described.

76

Our conversation about the war in Vietnam led to a story about Fort Franklin's involvement in World War II. Whaaaat? Yes, according to Travis, a German spy visited remote Fort Franklin in 1943. I can't see how that is possible, but Travis assures me the story is true. The spy was disguised as a missionary priest. He told the people in the village that he needed to go to Port Radium, a uranium mine on the other side of Great Bear Lake. One of the Dene men took the foreigner across the lake to the uranium mine.

However, the people in Fort Franklin were suspicious of the stranger who had come to their community. Some of the Dene informed the Royal Canadian Mounted Police that they didn't trust that man; they suggested that the RCMP investigate the intruder. The RCMP caught the spy just before he boarded a boat to return to Europe. When the RCMP searched the man, they found secret documents that he had stolen from the uranium mine. Imagine that kind of drama in a quiet little village far from the battlefront!

Remembering the uncanny way by which the people of Colville Lake were able to size up an individual, I am not surprised that the Fort Franklin Dene knew something was afoot when they met the foreigner in their community. But it's unsettling to learn of a uranium mine on the shores of pristine Great Bear Lake. Everyone knows that uranium ore is highly toxic ... right? I can't dismiss a vague sense of foreboding.

Travis and I spend long hours in conversation after everyone else has gone to their cabins for the night. Though he is reserved when we are in a group of people, my boyfriend can talk forever when we are alone together. I am spellbound by his stories. He remembers being born! Travis says he dimly recalls going through a dark tunnel toward a bright light.

Another of Travis' stories demonstrates the Dene knowledge of nature's ability to heal. While we were talking one evening, Travis pulled up his pant leg to show me a nasty red scar running halfway down his calf. Two years ago, he was hunting with a group of Dene men in the bush far from Fort

Franklin. The hunters had stopped to make camp, and Travis was tasked with chopping down saplings to use as tent poles. The axe slipped, slashing his leg wide open. The older men immediately sprang into action when they realized the extent of Travis' injury. Peeling off the bark of a spruce tree, they removed a white liquid from the trunk and spread it all over Travis' wound. Then the Elders wrapped the wound tightly and told Travis to rest without moving his leg.

Travis' return trip to Fort Franklin strapped to a dog sled was agonizing. Pain shot through his body with every jolt of the dog sled. Three days later, when the boy finally arrived at the hospital in Inuvik, the doctors found that his wound was perfectly clean. Stitches were not necessary because the lacerated flesh was already knitting together. I guess the spruce gum acted as a natural antibiotic.

Discussions with Travis reveal a way of thinking that is a far cry from anything I have ever known. He says, "I can only tell you what I know. I cannot ever judge another person. I cannot tell someone else what to do. I can only say who I am and how I live my life." Another time, he tells me, "I'm not too good at making plans. Just meet me under the sky somewhere and be alive with me."

With every conversation I am more strongly attracted to this quiet, gifted musician. Travis is funny, humble, sensitive and polite, embodying everything I have come to love about the Dene. His keen intellect coupled with genuine curiosity has won my heart. He respects his older brother, who teaches me about the complex, interconnected features of the North – grizzly bears, muskeg, tundra, permafrost, waterfowl, fish and myriad other elements of the Great Bear Lake ecosystem. I admire these brothers so much. They are entirely different yet their fraternal bond is strong.

Travis speaks English fluently, though he tells me he can express himself more fully in his first language. I wish I could understand his language so I could truly see the world through his eyes. I am beginning to discern a system of thought created by a consciousness far removed from my middle-class upbringing. For example, Travis knows the land and the lake far better than I know the streets of Edmonton. His life is in tune with natural cycles and the rhythms of the seasons. This strong and thoughtful person is exactly the kind of man that I have always dreamed of falling in love with.

I tell my Dene boyfriend about my failed experience in Colville Lake and end my complaint by trailing off, "I didn't accomplish what I wanted to. It's the story of my life ..."

Travis responds with a smile, "Never mind. You are the life of my story."

Hmmmm ... seems he might have some tender feelings toward me. That would be nice!

I'm curious about Dene terminology, grammar and syntax. Travis gladly explains some of the nuances of the fascinating language. He tells me that the order of words in his language is reversed. English sounds backward to him. We say, "Good morning," but the translation into Slavey is closer to "Morning good." Often his translations strike me as really funny. "It's even funnier in my own language," he says. "Sometimes I feel like I am almost a different person when I speak English."

The term for 'white man' seems peculiar to me. Travis explains that the Dene people named the white man *Ewie-daet-tını*, meaning 'those who carry death.' The Dene noticed that, wherever white people go, native people start dying from sickness. Influenza brought by fur traders caused epidemics that decimated the Dene population less than a century ago. The Elders concluded that sickness is carried by white people, hence their name. The explanation reminds me of the tragic history of smallpox and other diseases. I tell Travis that I have read about entire tribes in North America wiped out by diseases brought to the New World by European colonizers.

We share a devotion to the Catholic faith but, unlike me, Travis sees the entire world through a spiritual lens. He advises me, "You need to let go of everything ... everything.

Our life here on earth is only for a short while. Do what you can, and the rest is up to the Creator."

Then my sweetheart gently touches the tiny silver cross that hangs on a thin chain around my neck. A gift for my First Holy Communion ten years prior, the little cross is my only jewelry. "This is very powerful," he says. "I'm glad you wear it. The cross will protect you."

Travis tells me how he learned the doctrine of the Holy Trinity. "An Elder explained it to me this way," he says. "When you haul water from the lake in the winter, you first brush away the snow. Then you chisel down through the ice. Finally you put your bucket in the water. All three are different forms of the same thing. The snow, the ice and the liquid are all the same substance, but they seem different to us because they are not like each other. The Creator is like that. The Father, the Son and the Holy Ghost are just different shapes of the same spirit."

In Catholic school, I had learned the Irish legend which holds that St. Patrick explained the concept of the Holy Trinity through a shamrock. Now a universal symbol of Ireland, St. Patrick used the little green plant as a metaphor to describe the Trinity. The patron saint of Ireland showed that the three leaves on a shamrock are connected by a common stem, just as three persons are part of one God. I like the Dene explanation of the Holy Trinity because it makes sense in the Arctic context.

One evening, after Travis and the other guides have had a dispute with the lodge manager, I can see that my boyfriend is upset. "Travis, tell me what happened." I want him to talk about the altercation. Travis looks down at the ground and quietly says, "Let me get myself back first." That perfectly describes how I feel after an emotional blow-up. How can this young man be so eloquent when English is his second language? He must be REALLY intelligent.

Travis also tells me about some prophecies that were made by Elders in Fort Franklin many years ago. "An Elder said that one day the land will be like a checkerboard. Instead of forest and bush, the land will be carved up into squares. Not sure what that means."

"I think I know," I quickly reply. "When I flew north of Edmonton, I looked down on the farmyards and fields. They are all fenced off neatly in squares like a checkerboard. Maybe that's what the prophet could see."

I wonder how the Deline Elders in the far North who had never seen the land from an airplane could possibly imagine the appearance of the prairie farms in Alberta. Long ago, my dad told me that some people believe the Dene are descended from the lost tribes of Israel. Maybe the Dene also have prophets similar to the ones I learned about in the Bible. Conversations like this keep me and Travis up late every night.

Looking out over Great Bear Lake one evening, I say to Travis, "It is so huge … it's like the ocean." "What does that mean – the ocean?" he asks. Surprised, I turn to my friend. "How could you not know about the ocean? It covers most of the planet."

Travis looks off into the distance. "I only went to school for a few years," he replies simply. "My dad didn't want me and my brothers going away from home to residential school, so he took us out to the bush and hid us when the government people came to collect the kids."

"I don't know what you are talking about. What do you mean by residential school?" I ask.

Carefully, my boyfriend explains what happened to him as a child. The government told the people in Fort Franklin that their children needed an education. Because Fort Franklin was such a small community, boys and girls who lived there had to leave their community. They were taken away to attend school in larger centres like Inuvik and Aklavik, where they would stay for many months, far from their homes and families.

"My dad took my mom and all of us kids out into the bush where the government workers could not find us. He knew the government workers would take us away and he wanted us to stay with our family instead of going far away to live among strangers."

With Travis' revelation about residential school, the arrival of the little kids on the plane at Colville Lake suddenly begins to make sense. One day while I was at Colville Lake, a DC-3 landed on our little dirt runway. As always, everyone ran up the hill to greet the arrivals. I remember that day clearly because I was puzzled by the behaviour of the Dene women.

Strangely, the mothers had left their steaming pots and open fires to meet the plane. Even more strangely, only six children disembarked from the aircraft. One adult, a white man, accompanied them but he didn't stay more than a few minutes. The plane departed immediately after discharging the passengers. The young girls and boys, aged about eight to ten, looked lost and frightened. They stood in the sunlight on the landing strip, blinking and looking around warily. I didn't recognize the children, but the women in Colville were babbling in Slavey, sobbing unconsolably and reaching out to clasp the children tightly. These must be their children, but where did they come from?

Now the realization dawns on me. Travis' description of residential school explains the sudden arrival of children in Colville Lake. The kids on the airplane had been staying far away at residential schools. They were returning home for the summer. No wonder those little boys and girls looked confused and fearful. No wonder their parents were crying. Those poor children had been away from home for almost a year; it must have been terribly disconcerting for them to return to their tiny community, where everything was different – the language, the food, the people and the living conditions.

Travis went on telling me about his school experiences. "Later, a school was started in our community. The teachers were really strict with us kids. One time, a teacher threatened my dad, so my dad threatened the teacher."

"Tell me what happened," I beg him.

"The teacher had strapped me and my brothers for misbehaviour, so my dad took us out of school. When he did that, the government cut off our family allowance money. The teacher came to our house one day. He wanted to take us back to the school, but my dad said, 'No.'"

"The teacher argued with my dad and they both got angry. The teacher yelled at my dad, saying, 'I'm going to get my gun and come after you.'"

"My dad answered, 'Go ahead. Do it. I also have a gun.' That teacher never came back to the house. Ten years later, my dad told me, 'I'm still waiting for that teacher. Ha, ha!'"

My world view is rapidly changing through conversations with such an intriguing young man. He makes me think about everything differently. "Do you have a word for 'I'm sorry' in the Dene language?" I ask my friend one day. "I've never heard a Dene person say, 'I'm sorry'."

"Ummmmm …" I could tell he was thinking, so I didn't rush him. A few minutes later, Travis was still silent, mulling over different situations and how to respond appropriately in the Dene language. "I don't think so," he finally answered. And then, decisively, "No. We don't have a word to say 'sorry' in our language."

"Well, then, how do you express regret? I mean, if you do something to someone and then later you feel bad that you did it, what do you say?"

"We don't say anything. We just go over to that person and spend some time together. Just hang out. Be with him. We don't need to say something. We just need to be together."

These revelations feel like sacred confidences. I fall into bed every night reflecting on our conversations and promising myself that I will hold them in my heart forever. Copious notes in my diary can't possibly capture the essence of my experiences.

*

"Keep working!" Rosa yelled at me. The head cook was watching me with hawk eyes. Well, I hadn't stopped buttering bread for sandwiches, not even for a minute. But maybe my mind had wandered a bit, maybe I had smiled remembering last night around the bonfire, maybe I wasn't moving quite as fast as I should.

"Okay, okay," I laughed. "Lots of time before the guides pick up the shore lunches and head out to the boats." A scowl in my direction, and Rosa turned her attention back to the hot grill.

Wiping greasy hands on my apron, I turned to Karen, grabbed some sliced cheese from her and started slapping it on the bread. The other girls were serving guests the final cups of coffee in the dining room, stacking breakfast dishes for washing, and clearing tables, while Karen and I prepared lunch buckets with sandwiches, apples, juice and cookies. In a few minutes, the fishing guides would arrive at the kitchen door to pick up their shore lunches.

"Which lunch bucket is for Travis?" I whispered to Karen. "Right here," she answered with a grin. Quickly I slipped a little note under the bag of sandwiches in Travis' lunch kit. Karen was in on our secret, but no one else noticed the slip of paper wedged between two apples. I couldn't help smiling when I thought of Travis opening the lunch kit in a few hours' time to find the note from me, complete with a heart and happy face. Wonder what my beau will tell his guest?

Minutes later, Ted arrived at the door. The handsome twenty-year-old had completed his first year at the University of Alberta and was now guiding at Great Bear Lake to earn money over the summer. With neatly combed blonde hair and clear blue eyes, Ted's classic good looks were matched only by his generous spirit. The clean-cut lad planned to be a dentist, and he was the life of the party after hours when the guides and servers sat around the bonfire, telling jokes and singing songs. Following closely on Ted's heels came Andrew, Gordon, Drew, Lloyd and ten other young skippers on their way to help their guests catch the biggest fish in Great Bear Lake that day.

"Hope you catch a big one today!" "Be good to your guest!" "Don't fall overboard!" Karen and I had a grin and a comment for each guide as we handed them their lunch buckets. By looking down *at the sandwiches, I was able to keep my composure as Travis reached out for his lunch kit. Still, when I glanced up for a minute, our eyes met in an unmistakable exchange of raw emotion. He looked at me with a hint of longing gleaming in his dark eyes. I bit my lip and hoped no one was watching us.*

*

Sitting around the bonfire every night, the young men and women working at Trophy Lodge bond with each other. We sing songs by the Beatles, Simon and Garfunkel, the Carpenter Family, Neil Diamond and Creedence Clearwater Revival. While Travis and the other guitar players pick out the tunes, we make up our own words to the songs. No one cares if we are off key. All good fun.

Part of Travis' sex appeal is his large, capable hands with their perfectly formed fingers. It seems as if he can do anything he puts his mind to with those hands – strum chords, chop wood, string fishline – I want to feel those hands on my body!

Walking in the bush with Travis one day, he grabs my hand and helps me clamber over a fallen log. Then it just seems natural that we would keep holding hands. When he laces his fingers in mine, my heart surges. I feel confident walking through the bush with my hand in his. He seems so strong and calm. I like looking into his sparkling brown eyes and I learn so much from him. I care deeply about his brother, John. But I like Travis in a different way. Thinking about this young man makes my heart race. He is really smart, speaks two languages fluently, knows his way around the bush, gets along with everyone, keeps to himself but is easy to talk to – all qualities that I admire greatly … sigh …

Our first kiss captivates me. We are sitting around the campfire alone, long after everyone else has gone to bed for the night. I'm watching Travis as he strums his guitar. A final chord, and he places the instrument on the ground, balancing it carefully against the log beside him. Then, putting his arm around my shoulders, Travis looks down at me. Long, black eyelashes frame dark eyes that gleam with desire.

I close my eyes, he leans over and our lips meet in a lingering kiss. When I open my eyes, I see my man looking into my soul. I shiver with delight, savouring the sensation. Tasting his lips again, I feel my body curve into his of its own accord. Travis pulls me closer, crushing my breasts to his chest.

That's how Travis and I fell in love under the light of the midnight sun. Looking back, I see it now as a sweet, innocent love. We only wanted to be together, holding hands, singing, walking through the bush and talking about life. Being with him made me wildly happy and strangely contented at the same time. Little did I know that not everyone approves of a romance between a white girl and a Dene man.

7   The Moment

Ever since that first kiss and the promise of more to come, I can't stop thinking about Travis. He cast a spell over me – or something. I just know that he is different from anyone I have ever met. I want to learn as much as possible about his culture, traditions, language, relatives, history, friends … everything. I love listening to stories about his childhood growing up in the bush and learning to trap, hunt, fish and live off the land. Besides being nice to look at, he's a talented guitar player and an excellent fishing guide. He's kind, warm-hearted, smart, hard-working and soooo funny. We're always laughing together. Everything good in a person is in Travis. I want to live in Fort Franklin so I can get to know his mom, dad and his other brothers and sisters.

Sometimes I feel like I am enchanted, helpless under the spell of Travis' hands and lips. No, not helpless. I'm actually really busy. Up early every morning to serve breakfast to the guests, then clean the rooms, make the beds, scrub the floors, do the laundry – at Trophy Lodge, the workday begins at 6 am and doesn't end until very late in the day.

One day I am serving soup to a table of four. One of the guests looks directly at me. I can see he has been thinking about something. "Are you an Indian, Mary-Anne?" When I laugh and toss my head, my long braids almost touch the hot contents of his bowl. Gotta be more careful next time. I think the guests have been talking about me. Maybe I am not as polite or well-mannered as the other young ladies. I hope the manager wasn't watching our interaction.

Everyone in the camp seems to get along well but I sense an undercurrent of tension in the employees. The guides, in particular, are divided along racial lines. The white workers still eat dinner separately from the Dene who laugh and talk in their own language. I've been here a month and I am still the only white person sitting at the Dene table. Maybe there are unwritten expectations of me as a non-Dene. It just seems natural for me to gravitate to the native guides after spending two months with their confreres in Colville Lake. I can't tell if the white staff members are critical of my behaviour or if I am disturbing their routines. Perhaps my presence has upset some kind of delicate balance between natives and whites. Very puzzling. No one says anything to me, so maybe it's all right for me to spend time with the Dene. I still feel uneasy for some reason.

The Dene / white power dynamics are even more evident when the employees have been drinking after work. I'm not sure where all the booze is coming from, but beer and hard liquor flow freely around the blazing campfire. The guides often drink to excess and have been chastised by the management more than once for smelling of alcohol at the morning meeting. I have never acquired a taste for liquor and I especially dislike beer, so I am usually the only staff member who is completely sober when we finally turn in for the night.

I am startled one evening when a Dene guide suddenly jumps to his feet, enraged and shaking his fist. George is furious because he thinks one of the white guides was laughing at him. I thought we were all just having fun around the campfire, but something has infuriated our friend. When George threatens to punch Andrew, the young white man jumps up, ready to fight back. We are all afraid of what might happen if these two strong men start brawling. Luckily, the other guides calm down both men and we relax again. Although our companions did not exchange blows, the interaction was intense and heated. What is behind that kind of animosity?

The altercation is duly reported to Don, the manager of the guides, and the next day he calls all of us together to reprimand us in an angry lecture. During his verbal attack, he accuses us of being racist. Bewildered, I don't understand why he is blowing up at the employees. Advocating on behalf of the guides, Ted tries to explain their actions, only to then be accused by Don of drinking, partying and generally slacking off. As the conflict escalates, the young Dene men are noticeably silent. Why don't they defend themselves? No one speaks up on their behalf. The Dene guides merely sit, impassive, throughout the meeting. Like the people of Colville Lake, the Dene men prefer to avoid confrontation while the white guides are eager to discuss the situation. Naturally, the non-Dene dominate the meeting.

The racial divide is apparent to me, though it is foreign to my nature. Am I the only one who notices the contrast between white and Dene power dynamics? Socially and culturally, even linguistically, the groups have very different ways of interacting. The meeting concludes with hurt feelings and bitter words from staff and management. We are all feeling low when we return to our bunks. No bonfire tonight. No music. No lighthearted banter.

Karen, Cheryl and I converse quietly as we get ready for bed. There is a negative atmosphere running through our camp that I find disconcerting. I can't quite put my finger on the problem, but tensions are running high. Don is not the only one who is uptight these days. We agree that Lynn, the manager of the girls, seems stressed too. She snaps at us for no apparent reason. What are we doing wrong? Maybe we are still short-staffed. We are not sure what is driving Lynn's barbed comments and incessant demands on the servers. I wonder if I am seen as a troublemaker because of my interactions with the Dene.

The guides can escape the negative atmosphere in the lodge because they spend their days on the lake with their guests, but the female staff are under constant pressure from our manager. We are all working diligently; still, the kitchen is never quite clean enough to meet Lynn's standards. The windows must be spotless, the towels hung just so, the linens fluffy, the floors washed, the cutlery perfectly placed on the dining room tables. Seems that our efforts are never quite good enough to satisfy our manager. The problem might be me. Is my behaviour a disruptive influence in the camp? Maybe I am doing something wrong … am I too impatient? Too impulsive? Too outspoken?

I find the situation particularly challenging because the setting at the lodge is such a far cry from the dusty tents of Colville Lake where I savoured drinking black tea from chipped cups with my Dene friends. We didn't need running water or electricity because we were content with a simple lifestyle. My weekly hair-wash resulted in water that was grey with dust. At Colville Lake, I only washed my clothes every two weeks. Here at Trophy Lodge, we are constantly doing laundry. I have now spent six weeks in this fancy environment and the initial thrill has worn off. The focus on hygiene and elegant appearances is beginning to feel tedious.

Another thing that chafes at me is the resort policies. Rules imposed on us by the lodge managers seem ridiculous. Why shouldn't girls be allowed in the guides' bunkhouse after hours? Karen, Cheryl and I often sneak over for a harmless visit with Ted, Travis and George. We have been chastised more than once but that doesn't stop us. We need some time to just be ourselves, and our visits take place after hours. We work hard and should be allowed some freedom. Sometimes I long for those carefree afternoons with my Colville Lake companions.

I am not the only one who resents the tiresome chores and restrictive codes of conduct. Every evening my fellow servers cheer when the last dish has been put away. Finally, we can head to the beach where we will sit around the campfire and commiserate with each other. Putting aside the day's stress, I chat with friends, sing *Kumbayah* and hold hands with my Dene boyfriend. My spirits lift, and I am oblivious to the barely discernible tension that separates natives and whites.

This afternoon, Travis and I went for a walk in the woods together. He told me he knows of a place where we can be alone. I was surprised because we are never really alone – there is always someone nearby. Everyone in the camp knows everyone else's business. As in Colville Lake, privacy is impossible. There are no secrets.

We walked along the lakeshore for quite a way and then cut into the woods. Little trails ran all over the place. Travis seemed to know where he was going. After hiking through the bush and around stunted trees, we came upon a small canvas tent in the middle of a clearing. The ashes of a campfire showed that someone had stayed here and cooked over an open fire. I could smell freshly cut spruce. Wow. I never knew this little place existed. Wonder how Travis knew about it?

Travis raised the tent flap and I looked inside. Fragrant spruce boughs lined the perimeter. Against the far wall of the tent, I could see a little cot with some grey blankets and a thin pillow on it. A few battered pots and pans on the dirt floor indicated that someone had eaten a meal here. The interior of the tent glowed with golden sunlight suffused by the canvas cover. I could hear insects buzzing outside. No other sound. No one around. We actually had some solitude – unheard of.

Travis led me over to the cot and sat down on the edge. With a smile, he patted the spot beside him, gesturing for me to be seated. I laughed and said, "This little bed is not big enough for two."

"Oh, yes, it is," Travis replied. His brown eyes flashed an invitation. "Let's see what we can do."

He lay down sideways on the cot and I snuggled in beside him. His body next to mine seemed natural yet exciting, warm and familiar, yet different today because we were alone. My head fit perfectly on his chest, my legs automatically wrapped around his, and I breathed in his essence. Being so close to him with no one around was somehow intoxicating. His skin, his breath, his chest … I looked up into those deep brown eyes and my inhibitions melted away. Willingly, I raised my lips to his. As soon as we started necking, I could tell that our afternoon rendezvous was something serious. I felt *different inside ... like a light had started deep inside me and was spreading through my body.*

Our kisses became more passionate and Travis started running his hands along my back and down my buttocks. Through my thin T-shirt, I could feel his muscles tighten. Powerful emotions surged through me. I felt happy and tingly and somehow urgent. My body was responding in ways I had never dreamed of. Even as I was being swept along by my feelings, a voice inside my head was saying, "You know you could get pregnant, Mary-Anne ... and then what?"

It took a great effort for me to push myself a little way apart from Travis and take a deep breath. With difficulty, I managed to croak out, "Travis ... nnn... nnnoo ... no." Instantly, he stopped kissing my neck, lifted his head and looked into my eyes. There my boyfriend could see my hesitation. After a moment, he put his arms around my shoulders and raised himself up off the cot away from me. "It's all right," he said. "I understand."

"Oh, Travis," I murmured. "I'm sorry... I just can't... I really like you... I just can't... not right now, anyway ..."

"Okay," he replied, brushing the hair off my face and kissing my forehead. Then he put his arm around me and repeated, "It's okay. Let's go back to camp."

One last quick kiss, and we emerged from our little enclave into the brilliant sunshine. Our return to the lodge was quiet. I was burning with passion but couldn't express my feelings. My mind swirled with conflicting thoughts and my cheeks flamed as I tried to compose myself. Together, we scrambled through the bush, climbed back over the logs, found our way to the beach and walked along the sandy shore, holding hands. Then Travis said something funny and I realized I could still laugh. Everything really was going to be okay.

When Travis and I got back to the main lodge, no one mentioned that we had been gone. We had been away from the others for less than an hour. I felt like something inside me had changed, but the camp was bustling along as usual. What a relief!

Tonight began as the perfect evening, and it ended as the most humiliating moment of my entire life. All the guides and servers were sitting around the bonfire, laughing, singing and drinking. There were Jill, Linda, Marilyn, Donna, Andrew, Benjie, Rae, Grant, Jo-Jo, Jim, George, Ron, Paulette, Sheryl, Karen, Ted, Mickie, Grant, Johnny, Joseph, Martin, John, Bill and of course, me and Travis. The manager of the guides, Don, was hanging around in the bushes near the campfire, watching us. Don didn't join our circle, but I guess he had to supervise the younger staff at all times in case something went wrong. Maybe he is still worried about the altercation a few days ago.

I wore a warm sweater and jacket over my jeans and T-shirt. Despite the long hours of sunlight, it was now mid-August and I felt a chill in the air. Yesterday, a light snowfall had dusted the trees around the lodge, wet snowflakes melting as they hit the ground. A cool breeze from the lake reminded us that parts of Great Bear Lake never lose their ice, even during the hottest summer days. Norman Wells, south of us, had four inches of snow today. Summer in the Arctic will soon end. By the time we head to bed around ten o'clock, the sky will darken for a few hours, marking the beginning of the transition to complete darkness in a few short weeks. All of the Trophy Lodge staff are determined to enjoy the evening sun while it is still high in the sky.

Travis was strumming John Denver love songs on the guitar and I was sitting beside him, singing along whenever I remembered the words. I watched the flames in the crackling fire. At one point, Travis put down his guitar, leaned over and kissed me tenderly before taking a swig of beer. I smiled back at my guy, happy that we were still okay despite the afternoon episode in the tent. No one else seemed to notice or care that we shared a kiss. I guess everyone saw our romance coming. We've been spending a lot of time together. We just like holding hands, walking through the bush and talking about life for hours at a time.

Tomorrow is the day that the guests will leave Trophy Lodge to return to their homes in the south. Thankful for the companionship and expertise of their fishing guides, many of our visitors present their guides with parting gifts of alcohol or cigarettes the night before their departure. Ron, an athletic university student who will soon return to studying business at the University of Alberta, has been given a bottle of Canadian Club rye whiskey from his grateful American guest. I was mildly curious about his gift. Unscrewing the top, Ron handed the bottle to me and said, "I know you don't like beer. This is something different. Give it a try."

I sniffed the whiskey and gagged. Ugh … foul stuff … disgusting. "Just try it," Ron urged me. "You will like it." Everyone sitting around the fire seemed to be laughing at me. Well, I guess I could sip a little bit of the amber liquid. What's the harm of tasting the liquor? Anything is better than the flavour of beer. I vaguely recall putting the bottle to my lips. After that, it's all black.

The next thing I remember, I was vomiting into a toilet back at the main lodge. It was 3:30 am. Karen and Cheryl were holding my head up and keeping my hair off my face in an attempt to keep me clean. The commotion had roused Lynn, our manager, who was furious. I looked up to see her staring at me and quivering with rage.

"You tramp!" she screamed at me.

Whaaaaat? Even through my drunken haze, I could not understand why she called me a tramp. I am probably the only virgin in the entire camp. Is it wrong for me to kiss a Dene man? What is she talking about?

"Don saw you kiss that Indian boy. You're a disgrace," Lynn hissed.

"No, she's not," my friends tried to defend me. "She can't help being drunk. She didn't know she was drinking straight rye. Besides, Mary-Anne and Travis are in love."

"Well, she's out of here," commanded Lynn viciously. "We can't have staff behaving like that at our lodge." Then she fired me on the spot. "Mary-Anne is on the plane to Edmonton tomorrow."

94

"Noooooooo! You can't do that!!!" the girls screamed. But I was beyond fighting. Too sick to hold up my head, I just groaned as my friends half-carried me back to the cabin and tucked me into my bunk. Then everything went black again.

This was not the first time that a guide or chambermaid had been drunk, so why was I fired? It didn't seem real. Many of the guides had been drunk, got into fights and showed up at the lodge in the morning with a hangover, smelling of booze. None of them had been fired for drunk and disorderly behaviour. So why me? How could my employment at Trophy Lodge suddenly come to such an ignominious end? I tossed and turned on my bunk in a nightmare of humiliation. What would I tell my parents? Since there is only one flight a week into and out of the lodge, I had no choice. I would have to leave the next day.

Karen shook me awake the next morning. I moaned in pain. Now I know what a hangover feels like – the flu times ten. Why would anyone drink alcohol when it makes you feel this way? Throbbing headache, upset stomach, weak muscles, chills, shaking. Ugh. And, because of alcohol, I have to return to Edmonton. I don't really know what happened last night after I blacked out. I only know that I don't want to leave the North. I love my friends. I love the land, the wilderness, the people, the culture and the feeling of community. I'm learning the Dene language. I want to stay in the North with the Dene people. I don't want to go back to the city.

Oh no! A sudden thought occurs in my groggy brain – what about Travis? When I think of my handsome Dene boyfriend, I feel my heart breaking. All hopes of a future together are dashed. Pretty sure I would have married Travis and stayed up North for the rest of my life. We would have had such beautiful babies … I wanted to have eight children, all with black hair, brown eyes and sunkissed skin. How can I leave our shared dreams behind without any explanation?

I haven't fully processed my circumstances yet. But there is no time to think about what I am losing. No chance to say goodbye to anyone except my dear roommate. Karen and I sob and hold each other tightly, but she has to get to work and I have to pack for the plane ride back to Alberta.

The guides are already out on the lake with their guests, so I have no time to explain to anyone what has happened. Still queasy, I throw my few belongings into the battered blue suitcase that has accompanied me on every leg of this journey. My throat constricts and I can hardly breathe. Between painful sobs, I scribble a note for Travis:

Dear Travis, I have to go back to Edmonton. I'm so sorry. I wish I could say good-bye in person. Please tell everyone goodbye from me. I'll always remember you. Please stay in touch. I hope and pray we will see each other again.   Love forever, Mary-Anne☺

After folding the paper, I walk along the wooden boardwalk to the guides' bunkhouse for the last time. I take a moment to look around at the familiar log walls and bunk beds; then I place the note to Travis on the table in the centre of the room. Travis would find my message when he returned from a long day guiding his new guest out on the lake. Choking back tears, I walk back to the bunkhouse, pick up my worn suitcase and make my way along the uneven boardwalk to the dock where the float plane is waiting to take me back to civilization.

8   So This is Civilization

My stomach heaves as I climb into the single engine C-64 Norseman on floats, rocking against the wooden dock. The smell of avgas (aviation gasoline) nauseates me. Beyond the sheltered bay, I see whitecaps on Great Bear Lake. It's going to be a windy flight. Groan. That means turbulence – just what I don't need.

One glance at my distraught face and the pilot looks away, understanding without words that some calamity has transpired overnight. My shame is public because everyone knows I have done something disgraceful to be dismissed from the lodge before the end of the season. Grimly, I settle into my seat and buckle up.

The 750-mile flight from Great Bear Lake to Yellowknife is torturous. I huddle in the cramped space, alternately crying and heaving into a paper bag. My world has been shattered and the loss seems unbearable. Oblivious to the subtle tensions separating camp staff into Dene and white, I had failed to detect the ugly undercurrent of racism. Now I am paying the price. I am profoundly disappointed in myself, ashamed of my actions and sick at heart. After four gut-wrenching hours aloft, we land at the float dock in Yellowknife. There, I transfer to the airport and a larger plane which will take me on a four-hour commercial flight to my final destination back in Edmonton. From the moment I leave the creaky wooden dock on Great Bear Lake, I am surrounded by strangers, lost, alone and vulnerable without my Dene friends to nourish my spirit.

As the aircraft heads south over the immense sapphire water of Great Slave Lake, sobs wrack my body. This is farewell to the North. Farewell to unending sunlight, crystal clear lakes, fish, caribou steaks, moose hide, log cabins and canvas tents. Worst of all, I am parting from the gentle, funny, wise, copper-skinned people who had become so dear to me. Would I ever again see my Dene friends or the young man I had begun to love so deeply?

I think about the five Dene communities I had visited: Fort Norman, Norman Wells, Fort Good Hope, Colville Lake and Fort Franklin. Would I ever return? Looking down from my vantage point on the plane, I see only massive bedrock, willows, tamarack, birch trees and lakes puddled on the landscape. Then the vast, green boreal forest unfolds below the plane, as far as the eye can see. A few hours later, neat squares of cultivated fields begin to appear. Was it only four months ago that I saw them from the air for the first time? Seems like a lifetime has passed since I flew to Yellowknife on a wing and a prayer. So much has changed since then. My dream of living with the Dene has crashed, and I have no idea what lies ahead.

My eyes follow undulating rivers and arrow-straight prairie roads until the outskirts of Edmonton come into view. A strange sensation comes over me when I see large buildings and paved roads. The eerie feeling intensifies when I witness the sun setting and dusk falling outside the aircraft. The twilight seems alien to me. Deep breaths. I can do this.

Even with a nonstop flight from Great Bear Lake to Yellowknife and another direct flight from Yellowknife to Edmonton, the trip home took almost 12 hours. The aircraft lands in Edmonton at 10:30 pm in late August, a time when the sun is still bright in the high Arctic. Disembarking from the plane, I see complete darkness for the first time in 15 weeks. After experiencing continuous daylight for so long, the vast, empty black sky is unnerving.

Worse than the darkness are the electric lights which light up the night sky in a weird juxtaposition. And the noise ... cars honk, trucks roar past and an ambulance screams in the distance. The stark contrast with the quiet bush camp is bizarre and confusing, but the worst is yet to come. When I finally reach my parents' house, I see rows of houses in a straight line, all featuring locked doors and curtained windows. I realize that I am anonymous here in the city. I need to have a reason for knocking on someone's door. Instead of freely coming and going as we did in the Dene community and at Trophy Lodge, everyone in this urban centre lives under lock and key. I am back in the booming metropolis of Edmonton. The return to 'civilization' shocks me to my core.

'Fragmented' is the word that comes to mind. My soul is in pieces. I feel disconnected. Cut off. Isolated. Where is my community? Where are my friends? The cold, dark, anonymous environment numbs me. I want to smell spruce needles again and breathe the fresh air blowing off the lake. I want to hear people speaking the Dene language. I want to laugh for no reason and go fishing in pure, untouched water. I do not want concrete and pavement and strangers.

This is culture shock – big time. I am 'bushed.' I have come from tents and log cabins to skyscrapers and convenience stores, from endless sunshine to pitch-dark nights bristling with tall lamp standards. The transition is disquieting. Living close to nature instinctively felt right, but the artificial environment of the city seems somehow hostile.

I still feel sick to my stomach and my head is pounding. I can't talk to my parents or siblings about my dismissal from the lodge. They won't understand my dashed hopes for a future where I would teach children in the North. Emotional and physical exhaustion renders me mute, my anguish palpable. Respecting my silence, my family gives me space.

Just a few months ago I had been a carefree teenager. Now I feel older, stung by defeat, my spirit crushed. Conflicting thoughts swirl in my head. What had I done to be banished from the lodge? Why did the manager hate me? Just when I had found some direction in my life, everything turned topsy-turvy. I have lost my way again. There is no one I can talk to, no one to turn to.

My good intentions had resulted in only heartache. Going up North had been a colossal mistake. I should have just stayed home and worked around Edmonton for the summer. Instead of serving the First People of Canada, I had imposed on the goodwill of the missionary. Then I had embarrassed myself and brought shame on my family by getting drunk. The only good thing about the entire summer was my Dene boyfriend, yet I would probably never see him again. When my mother inquires gently about my summer experience, I am unable to respond. No one in the world could possibly understand what I have been through and how I feel. I try to carry on as if everything is normal. But the world has changed irrevocably for me. My life has unravelled and I have no idea how to stitch it back together.

Alone in my bedroom at last, I pray as best I can for deliverance from the emotional torment I endure. In addition to feeling like I have failed in my quest to serve the Dene, I miss my new love, my friends and life on the lake in the wilderness. How can I cope with the noise and bustle of Edmonton after the freedom of bush life? I am an outsider again, this time in a weird world called a city. Returning to such an artificial environment feels terribly wrong.

In my wallet, two wrinkled one-dollar bills and a few coins are all that remain of my original $38. I unpack my few belongings from the now-shabby suitcase. After tucking my diary into a desk drawer, I clutch the treasured mementoes I have brought home – a caribou hide purse and moccasins sewed for me by Sarah back in Colville Lake.

I long for the aroma of wood smoke, the children's laughter, the open doors, the dried fish, the never-ending sunlight, the lake, the caribou meat, my Dene beau. In an effort to alleviate the ache in my heart, I bury my nose in my moose-hide slippers and rub my cheeks against the beaver-fur trim. Instead of talking about my experience, I will try to forget what happened and instead put the past behind me. Maybe if I don't think about it, the pain will go away.

But those flashing brown eyes, that husky Dene voice, the guitar chords – it's hard to banish Travis from my mind and my heart. I ask myself over and over how things could have turned out differently. I fall asleep that first night wondering why I had been torn away from the man who had captured my heart.

100

The first thing I do the next morning is to write a letter. Hoping it will somehow make it to Fort Franklin and then to Travis himself, I pour out my soul. I write and tear up a dozen drafts before I finally find the words to express my feelings. Then I agonize over how to sign it – I can't remember what I wrote in the note I left him at the lodge. Do I dare sign it: *Love, Mary-Anne*? Everything has changed now. Maybe I should write: *Your friend, Mary-Anne*. Definitely not: *Sincerely*.

Dear Travis, Well, I'm back in Edmonton and really miss the North. Really miss you, too. You know how much I wanted to stay in the North and go to university and then teach in Fort Franklin. But I guess it wasn't meant to be. I've been thinking about you and the good times we had together. Wish you were here to play guitar and talk to me. Lonely in the city. I found a picture for you. Hope I will see you again one day.   Xoxoxo, Mary-Anne ☺

Into the envelope I tuck a small black-and-white portrait of my face laughing into the camera, freckles dancing across my nose and long auburn hair tumbling down past my shoulders. After I seal the envelope, I have a sudden thought. I dab on some lipstick, then press my lips against the envelope, leaving a perfect imprint of my lips on the seam. Nice! He will like that. A five-minute walk takes me to the mailbox where I drop my missive with a little prayer that the message will eventually reach my sweetheart in far-off Fort Franklin.

Despite being sick at heart, I have plenty to do over the next two weeks before the first day of classes at the University of Alberta. Registering for university and finding part-time work is time-consuming, requiring long days of phone calls, application forms, job interviews and bus rides. I pine for my fun-loving roommate, but I don't have the courage to look up my Trophy Lodge friends in the phone book. Instead, I desperately want to forget that the ugly incident had ever happened. My evening prayers are devoted to fervent requests to somehow get my life back on track.

I recall with nostalgia the easy companionship of my friends in Colville Lake and Trophy Lodge and wonder if I will find new friends at the university. The summer had begun with a flurry of excitement and ended in disappointment. I wonder if I am on the right path now. Maybe I am doing myself more harm than good, flitting around from place to place, from job to job. Sometimes I feel like I am a square peg in a round hole. Will I ever belong with someone somewhere?

Gazing into the distance over Great Bear Lake (photo courtesy of Morris Neyelle, 2016).

The first day of university brings an unexpected ray of sunshine into my world. A handsome young professor who is clearly passionate about anthropology introduces himself and explains the upcoming syllabus. Looks like the course will be thought-provoking. I'm intrigued. Then, ten minutes before the end of class, our instructor springs a surprise on me and my classmates. For the first time, the University of Alberta Faculty of Education is hosting students from the Northwest Territories who plan to become teachers. Our teacher wants us to welcome Bobby Overvold from Fort Good Hope and Ethel

Blondin who has come all the way from the tiny village of ... Fort Franklin!

A tall, strikingly beautiful young woman stands up, grins and waves at the class. Long, thick, copper-coloured hair cascades halfway down her back. A generous smile and sparkling brown eyes light up the distinctive Dene features of her face. Ethel Blondin is the answer to my prayers, a tangible link with my recent northern experience. Such an unforeseen coincidence buoys my flagging spirits.

After class, I quickly catch up to Ethel in the hallway. "Are you related to Jo-Jo Blondin?" I blurt out. Ethel looks at me incredulously. "Of course! Jo-Jo is my cousin. But how could you possibly know Jo-Jo Blondin? He lives in Fort Franklin, a million miles from Edmonton."

Excitedly, I explain the Fort Franklin connection and name the Dene guides who had befriended me at Trophy Lodge. Ethel was born in Fort Norman and grew up in Fort Franklin. She is well-acquainted with all the Trophy Lodge fishing guides. The vivacious twenty-year-old explains some of the intricate family connections among the people of the Sahtu and tells me stories from her childhood on Great Bear Lake. Our conversation flows effortlessly and we make plans to meet again the next day.

Ethel and I quickly become fast friends. Both of us have been raised in poverty and know how to make a few dollars go a long way. Having survived tuberculosis and other major illnesses, Ethel has a philosophy of life that is much more mature than her chronological age. She is truly an 'old soul.' In 1959, when Ethel was only eight years old, she was sent from her home in Fort Franklin to Grolier Hall in Inuvik, one of the residential schools that Travis had mentioned. My new friend later studied at Grandin College in Fort Smith, in a unique program designed to prepare Indigenous youth for leadership roles. Like me, this ambitious brunette planned to return to the North to teach the Dene. Unlike me, Ethel has three youngsters to care for, in addition to an equally rigorous schedule of studies.

I am thrilled to find someone who shares my dream of teaching in the North and more than happy to spend time with Ethel's adorable children. Her wicked Dene sense of humour keeps our spirits high during long days of classes and long nights of writing essays.

Thanks to typing classes in high school, I had acquired superior typing skills and took great pride in my speed and accuracy – almost 100 words per minute, with no errors. Thus, transcribing Ethel's essays on to her little portable Remington Rand typewriter is a breeze for me. We bond over tea, cinnamon rolls and long philosophical discussions sparked by our university courses.

Over the next two years of university, Ethel and I become closer than sisters. She is one of only a handful of people who refer to me by my childhood nickname, 'Mio.' We even share household duties at her little apartment. I change baby Timmy's diapers while Ethel researches a topic. We make lunch together and police the two older children. Our conversations are often interrupted by one or more of the kids. Her husband, Ron, relaxes on the couch and occasionally joins our discussions with his own opinions.

Two years of university classes pass quickly. The sting of failure I had felt back in 1971 begins to lessen and finally disappears. Immersed in linguistics, literacy and First Nations studies, I soak up knowledge like a sponge. I am particularly absorbed in the anthropology classes. However, our anthropological studies are focused on the Haida and Tsimshian people of the Pacific Northwest or the Algonquin and Huron people of eastern Canada. I search the libraries and bookshelves in vain for current information about my Dene friends. That's when I recognize the need for researchers such as Joel and Susan Savishinsky who might begin to close that knowledge gap by publishing their findings.

When Ethel and I talk about our respective love lives, I tell her only that I had a crush on someone from her hometown. No details. The memories are still too painful. Instead, we focus on getting through our university courses. When this young mom is briefly hospitalized, I bring her flowers and help Ron look after the children until she recovers. I have no inkling that my dear friend will go on to a stellar career as the first Indigenous female Member of Parliament for the Western Arctic, admired by Canadians for her strong leadership. For now, we are just two university students struggling to get through the education program as best we can. The future is still a mystery.

Colville Lake, Fort Franklin and Trophy Lodge are the common bonds between me and Ethel, but I am much too busy to dwell on the past. Classes, assignments, interim employment and dating keep me fully occupied. Despite carrying a full schedule of university courses, I work at two part-time jobs to pay the bills. Every day is full. When memories of the North well up, unbidden, I do my best to quell them by burying myself deeper in work and socializing.

Life goes on and no one guesses my secret pain, secret heartache and secret sorrow. Deep down, I miss everything about my summer in the North, especially my Dene sweetheart. I mourn that two souls had connected oh-so-briefly and that our innocent love was unrequited. But such things happen. Time to move on with my life.

Still, in the back of my mind I am waiting for a letter, hoping to hear back from Travis. Did my Dene beau ever receive my picture and the message? Did he still feel the same way toward me? Was he still my boyfriend? As long months pass, I feel his memory slipping from my mind, like our fingers slipping apart. I try to forget those deep brown eyes burning into mine and that indescribable feeling of soul touching soul. Instead, I pour my energy into acquiring the skills and knowledge required to become an engaging English teacher.

As a university student, I am passionate about taking action. I especially want to share my new-found appreciation for the inner beauty of Indigenous people. I want someone to write a book that will celebrate people of First Nations descent throughout Canada. This book would depict the First People in the way that I think of them – as heroes to be admired and role models to be followed.

When I was a little girl, I loved reading *The Lives of the Saints*. My parents taught me that we should emulate the characteristics demonstrated by the saints – patience, kindness, compassion, generosity, forgiveness, courage, wisdom, modesty and selflessness. These were values that I saw in abundance among young and old during my time with the Dene. Maybe a book based on the lives of Indigenous Canadians would demonstrate their admirable character traits and motivate readers to embrace some of the ways of life that endeared the Dene to me.

I tell friends and teachers at the University of Alberta about my vision for a book that would honour Indigenous Canadians as the true heroes in our history. For some reason, everyone persists in calling Indigenous Canadians 'Indians,' as if they are all the same. My friends in Colville Lake have a totally different language and culture from the Cree in Alberta. I want to explain what I have learned first-hand. And I want to refer to my friends as 'Original' people, not Indians. Most of my textbooks now call the First People of North America 'Aboriginal,' but that doesn't seem right, either. The Latin prefix 'ab' means 'away from,' which is the opposite of this context. Why can't we call the people who were here before Europeans arrived 'Original'?

Professors and fellow students think a book honouring Indigenous Canadians is a great idea, but no one makes a move to shape that vague concept into a reality. Apparently, books about Aboriginal people have limited appeal. Still, I cling to that dream over the next half century and try many times to act on my intention. I desperately want to explain how the Dene had nourished my soul by just being themselves. I hope that my journey of understanding might shine a light on Indigenous ways of knowing and being. Dene wisdom might also illuminate non-Indigenous lives. But how can I write a book with competing demands on my time and energy? I keep putting off the project and prioritizing other, more urgent tasks.

All too soon, our university years come to an end. In 1973, Ethel and I part ways, vowing to remain friends forever. She heads back up North with her family to teach school in Tuktoyaktuk, even farther north than her hometown. Wistfully, I recall my brief visit to Fort Franklin, the little Dene community in the North where I had felt some kind of spiritual presence calling me. But it's just not practical for me to consider teaching in that remote settlement when my skills are needed in the province of Alberta.

With only a three-year teaching certificate under my belt, I am offered a position teaching high school English in northern Alberta. Time to make a decision. Having heard nothing from my former boyfriend in the Northwest Territories, I decide to start my teaching career in Mayerthorpe, located a hundred miles northwest of Edmonton in the County of Lac Ste. Anne. Instead of going up North, I will stay closer to home.

Ethel and I reconnect every summer for the following two years. We take summer school classes at the University of Alberta, where both of us earn full teaching credentials with Bachelor of Education degrees. After that, our friendship endures for more than fifty years.

9   Teaching

As a beginning teacher with the County of Lac Ste. Anne, I live off-the-grid on my father's childhood farm, located a mile south of the almost-ghost town of Rochfort Bridge and just a fifteen-minute drive to the Mayerthorpe school. Living off-the-grid means no electricity, no indoor plumbing, no telephone and, as I am soon to discover, no insulation in the walls to protect me from the intense cold of a prairie winter. Since Uncle Jimmy passed away a few years ago, no one is looking after the old homestead. It takes me a full day just to sweep away the desiccated remains of flies and spiders that have accumulated over time. An enormous vegetable garden keeps me busy hoeing weeds. I raise chickens for eggs and rabbits for meat. Teaching high school teenagers pays the bills.

Until the house is wired for electricity and telephone a month after I move in, I read at night by the dim yellow light of a coal-oil lantern. I rise early every morning to kindle a fire in the wood stove. Believe me, bringing water to a boil takes forever on a cold stove. My vain attempt to make popcorn one summer afternoon concludes with a very hot kitchen, a mess of cooked kernels and disappointed laughter from the ten-year-old neighbour I was hosting. I soon learn the vagaries of temperature control and become adept at cooking on a wood stove. Bread dough rises beautifully on the back of the stove and then bakes to golden perfection in the evenly heated oven.

The well water tastes of iron but is fresh and cold. I start the pump by pulling the rip cord for the gasoline engine. Soon water is splashing into my pails from deep underground. My arm muscles grow strong from hauling buckets of water daily from the pump house to the kitchen. As I had learned from living in a bush camp, lack of running water presents many challenges, especially for personal hygiene. Thankfully, the school principal allows me to shower in the girls' change room before school begins each morning. But at home, I freeze my bare bottom when I use the outhouse in the winter.

My first day of classes as a full-time teacher stretches me in every possible way. Once again, I feel that I have passed through a doorway into a different world. In this new role, others look to me for direction. Barely 21 years old, I do not feel like a leader. The Grade 12 English 30 class consists of 38 students who are only a few years younger than me. Not an Indigenous face to be seen. Every student has European ancestors. Many of their parents immigrated to Canada after World War II from Germany. Others came from the British Isles. The teenaged boys are clearly bored, and the teenaged girls just want to flirt with the boys. It seems impossible that I will ever be able to hold their attention for a full hour at a time.

I walk around the classroom holding a yardstick in my hand like a weapon. Although I don't threaten any of my students, I feel slightly more in control with a stick that I can point or whack on someone's desk if he is not paying attention. Every time I turn my back on my class to write on the chalkboard, I can only hope that the teenagers will refrain from throwing spitballs or worse. Somehow I manage to keep smiling throughout that interminably long day. It's after midnight when I fall asleep the first night, wondering if I will be able to sustain this pace until June.

During those early years of my teaching career, an English Language and Literature class of 35 – 40 students is not unusual. With only half an hour of prep time each week and two days off for professional development per year, I am fully occupied for at least 12 hours every day. Teacher training did not adequately prepare me for the daily grind. To develop lessons, teach classes, meet with colleagues and grade essays is far more time-consuming than I had ever dreamed.

Evenings and Saturday afternoons are for meeting with parents and my fellow teachers. Most of the students are below grade level in literacy. Many have special needs. Each one requires all the support I can provide. The concept of an

Educational Assistant to support the teacher has not yet been considered. The School District Superintendent explains that the summer months are to be spent on professional development, preparing lesson plans for the following year and organizing the classroom. I am expected to take no more than two weeks of vacation time during July and August.

Plunging into my teaching duties, I stubbornly bury the Arctic memories because it seems impossible to go back up North. "You can't step in the same river twice," according to an ancient Greek philosopher. That part of my life is definitely over. I have to move on.

Slowly, my dream of honouring the Dene through literature begins to slip away, replaced by the demands of a move to rural Alberta and a challenging teaching career. A brief abusive marriage ends with a black eye, leaving me penniless and emotionally devastated, bruised in body and soul.

After two years of living on a farm and teaching in a rural school, I return to Edmonton in 1975. The next stage of my teaching career takes place at St. Joseph Composite High School, a huge inner-city school with 2,600 students in grades 10-12. When I see the occasional Indigenous face in the hallway, I feel a pang of regret for the Dene I had left behind four years ago. I am drawn to the few Indigenous students who have surmounted formidable odds to make it to high school. Remembering the children of Colville Lake, I wonder if they are learning to speak English without me there to guide them. But, once again, teaching obligations take priority. There is nothing I enjoy more than inspiring a room full of teenagers to learn about the world through reading and writing. Grateful students write heartfelt letters of thanks, draw pictures for me, and tell me I have changed their lives forever. Life is good.

Digging the dirt

Home-grown veggies keep you and your budget healthy

MARY ANN
GILLESE

I wrote monthly features for the Lifestyle section of the *Edmonton Sun* from 1982-1985.

In 1976, I marry a University of Alberta graduate student; my teacher's salary pays the household bills. We are struggling financially but I long to start a family. The following year, I give birth to a son, Geoffrey. I am still teaching full-time and there are no provisions for parental leave in 1977. My colleagues assume that I will resign from my position so that I can become a full-time mother, but I persuade the Human Resources department at the Edmonton Catholic School Board to allow me to take two months of unpaid leave from work. I am grateful to the School Board for holding my position until I can find care for my newborn. Day care centres are unheard of, so I knock on doors in the neighbourhood until I find a woman with two children of her own who is willing to look after my baby boy while I resume my teaching duties. I am back in the classroom the day after my infant son turns two months old.

Three years later, Michelle is born and the marriage is crumbling. When my husband departs the country with another woman, I am left on my own to raise a newborn and a toddler. As full-time caregiver for my children, without child support or weekend relief, I am barely getting by financially and emotionally.

Modelling helped pay the bills when I was raising my first two children alone (1982). My infant and toddler accompanied me to every shoot; sometimes they modelled, too.

After six weeks of drawing unemployment insurance, my benefits run out. Part-time work as a model and a movie extra pays some of the bills. Writing lifestyle columns for the *Edmonton Sun* and *Edmonton Magazine* also helps. Occasionally, I narrate programs and voice-overs for Access Radio and Television Network. Through a local talent agency, I earn enough credits as a talent extra and writer to become a member of ACTRA, the Association for Canadian Television and Radio

Artists[15]. But the only way to keep the wolf from the door is to return to full-time work as a teacher.

This stage of my life is a hectic whirlwind of work and family, doing the best I can to raise my young children alone. To stave off the pangs of loneliness, I dedicate myself to my children and my career. Rising at 5:30 am, I prepare lunches, wake the children and get ready for a full day. I bundle the two of them into the car and we are out the door by 7:15 am. I am on my feet all day long, keeping crowded classes of teenaged boys and girls occupied with their studies, directing the choir, coaching badminton and supervising various school-sponsored activities. Classes of 35 students are still common and, with less than half an hour each day for lesson preparation, it's hard to find time to use the bathroom. I am grateful for two professional development days each year, two days off at Easter and ten days at Christmas. After school, I pick up Geoffrey and Michelle, make dinner, bathe them, sing them to sleep and spend an hour or two grading papers. 9:30 pm finds me falling into bed, exhausted, so I can do it all over again the next day.

Before tucking my children into bed each night, we say evening prayers together. We express gratitude for special moments that day, bless our loved ones and ask our heavenly Father to calm our fears and guide us. Evening prayers are a quiet time for the three of us to bond before I kiss my little ones good night and we fall asleep. Raising children alone is challenging, and spiritual meditation helps me feel a little less lost and confused.

By 1982, a few day-care centres have popped up in the city and I am lucky to find a spot for my baby girl. I pay a neighbour to escort Geoffrey to kindergarten and look after my little boy at her home until I can pick him up after school. Later, Geoffrey comes to my high school classroom in the morning

---

[15] Renamed Alliance of Canadian Cinema, Television and Radio Artists in 1986.

before his school day begins. My son quietly colours or reads while I am teaching. Weekends are a never-ending cycle of grocery-shopping, laundry and preparation for the coming week. Summer months are reserved for visiting relatives and friends, travelling to the mountains, gardening and generally enjoying precious time with my growing children.

I've never liked the anonymity of a big city and Edmonton expanded quickly during the 1970s. When the first phase of West Edmonton Mall opens in 1981, I realize that my hometown has become almost unrecognizable. Maybe a large metropolitan area is not the ideal place to raise my little family. I worry about negative influences on my youngsters as they grow up and venture out into the city. Alberta's oil boom has brought easy money and transient workers. The adolescents that I am teaching tell me horror stories about the pervasive influence of drugs and alcohol. In 1986, I begin to think that a smaller centre will provide Geoffrey, Michelle and me with a stronger sense of community and a more balanced lifestyle.

Teaching on-camera for the ACCESS Television Network show "Homework Hotline" in 1986.

When I was teaching in the country, I liked living on a farm because I knew everyone for miles around. Neighbours were more than acquaintances. We were allies. Farmers count on each other for advice and practical support such as help with childcare, gardening, animal husbandry and chores. As a single mom, I want to live in a tight-knit community where people care about their neighbours and watch out for each other. However, I also need a setting where I can find employment, preferably somewhere that the children can walk to school. After researching a few locations in Canada, I choose Victoria, capital city of British Columbia, as the best fit for me and my growing children.

Maybe a smaller centre will provide that connection and sense of inclusion that I had found in the remote northern communities so long ago when I was transitioning into adulthood. I begin to prepare for the big move away from my hometown, never dreaming that our resettlement on Vancouver Island would be fraught with setbacks that will test my mettle again and again.

10   Building a New Life

The next 35 years pass as if in a dream. Trying to rebuild my career in a strange new city without my professional network is harder than I thought, especially when I learn that there are no teaching positions available on Vancouver Island. In 1986, I had no access to the internet and had not researched the job market in Victoria. Naively, I had believed that I could easily land a job with my varied skill set. Wrong. The Assistant Superintendent of the Victoria School District tells me that I would have to work as a substitute teacher for at least ten years before a position might open up. No jobs in the media or modelling, either. All my sources of income have dried up. Without child support or alimony from my former husband, I am living off my meager savings and desperate to acquire paid employment so that I can provide for my children.

Where to live is another issue. Finding a place to rent as a single mom without an income proves to be a nightmare. People are courteous but I have few options. I don't blame the landlords for their lack of trust in a complete stranger who is jobless, with two children and no local references. Most days it's tough to keep a smile on my face. I begin to feel that I have lost my way again.

The last straw is a break and enter at our rented accommodation. My purse is stolen, along with my driver's license, credit card and all my identification. Alone, vulnerable and unsupported with two young dependents in a foreign environment, I don't know if I can handle any more setbacks. That's the week the local food bank in downtown Victoria helps us out. Somehow, my children and I get through the rocky times together.

On days when I am so emotionally drained I can hardly get out of bed, Geoffrey and Michelle never fail to lift my spirits. I am grateful for their laughter at my worries. "If we don't have any money, we can just go to the bank and buy

116

some money," reasons six-year-old Michelle innocently. Our relaxed lifestyle in a small community near the ocean somewhat compensates for the loneliness and lack of funds.

Geoffrey and Michelle walk to school every day, and the weather on Vancouver Island is so mild that they play outdoors all year long. Soccer season begins in September and runs right through until June. Sports, school and friends occupy the kids' time in healthy activities. Kind neighbours keep an eye on my little boy and girl while I search for work. I hold a succession of modest jobs that pay the bills and keep us in groceries. My nine-year-old son and I rise early every day to deliver morning newspapers together. Since I have never earned much in the way of an income, I can make a few dollars stretch a long way.

Our first Christmas in our new community is memorable for our Charlie Brown Christmas tree[16] and lack of gifts. I had only enough money to purchase a few necessities for Geoffrey and Michelle so that they would have something to unwrap on Christmas morning. Surprisingly, they both appear delighted to receive a new toothbrush, new tube of toothpaste and their very own bottle of chewable Vitamin C. It was only when I overheard my children talking to their friends that I realized they quickly changed the subject when it came to presents from Santa.

Somehow, our little family manages to scrape by year after year. Occasionally a whiff of wood smoke or the scent of spruce boughs awakens long-lost memories of the Sahtu, but nostalgia is quickly replaced by more immediate considerations such as peeling potatoes, paying bills or helping construct a class project with one of the children.

Meanwhile, my former classmate, Ethel Blondin, has achieved her goals both personally and professionally –

---

[16] An idiom referring to a thin, scraggly tree, based on the *Peanuts* character created by Charles Schultz. Charlie Brown chooses a sad-looking tree to decorate for Christmas.

personal happiness in her marriage to Leon Andrew and professional success in the political arena. After teaching in the North and holding increasingly more responsible posts in Ottawa and Yellowknife, she became an Assistant Deputy Minister for the Ministry of Culture in the government of the Northwest Territories. Then this exceptional woman decided to run for office in the federal government. Elected Member of Parliament for the Western Arctic in 1988, she became the first Indigenous woman to serve in Canada's House of Commons.

On Ethel's rare trips to Victoria, we are both overjoyed to see a face from our shared past. Although her visits are infrequent, Geoffrey and Michelle call my adopted sister 'Auntie Ethel,' and we all consider her and Leon to be part of our extended family. I am inordinately proud of this strong, spirited woman and more than happy to write speeches for Ethel to deliver at various official events during her 17 years in Parliament.

After 11 years as a single parent and a succession of disappointing relationships, I fall in love with a wonderful man. Kind-hearted and industrious, Mike works at an automotive shop and has been a bachelor until the age of 37, when he proposes to me. My new beau cherishes my son and daughter as his own. After we marry, I promptly give birth to another girl and then another boy. Our little family flourishes. In my life partner I have found a caring husband and father who immediately shoulders a large portion of household responsibilities. Together, Mike and I share the financial, physical and emotional challenges of raising a family. We share the joys, too. The rewards of being a mother stretch far beyond my wildest dreams. The challenges remind me that we are always learning and growing.

Every day is full – volunteering at the school, coaching soccer, substitute teaching, chauffeuring kids to play dates and spending weekends at Shawnigan Lake. When I attend church on Sunday, I pray for my Dene friends and wonder if they are saying the rosary in Our Lady of the Snows log chapel. Singing lullabies to my babies at bedtime, I sometimes feel a sharp pang, remembering nightly singalongs around the campfire at Trophy Lodge. These moments soon pass and I am back to the reality of diapers, mortgage payments, laundry, making meals and supervising homework.

In an effort to contribute what we can and cultivate a sense of social justice in our children, our little family joins Plan Canada, a charitable organization that provides food, clothing and school supplies for youth in developing countries. Through Plan Canada, we sponsor foster children in war-torn parts of the world. Every few months, we eagerly open letters from our sponsored children to learn about their lives so far away from us. Our five-year-old foster child in Sudan sends us a picture she has drawn of her neighbourhood. My children and I are horrified to see dead dogs bleeding in her street and airplanes raining bullets from the sky. This little girl's view of the world reminds us of our good fortune to live in a peaceful society.

Geoffrey, Michelle, Christina and Robbie keep me and Mike fully occupied around the clock. Each child is a unique gift with a fascinating combination of character traits. I feel blessed with the good fortune of caring for four beautiful souls during their formative years. My rock-solid partner is the glue holding us all together. Life is hectic and life is good.

When our youngest children are two and four years old, it's time for me to get serious about my career again. Best to build on my existing Bachelor of Education degree (with distinction) from the University of Alberta. Consequently, at age 45, I enroll in the Master of Education program at the University of Victoria. I hope to develop curriculum resources that will engage students of all abilities, and I want to learn about the emerging use of technology to enhance learning.

Geoffrey, Michelle, Christina and Robert in front of our home in Victoria, BC (2004).

Two years later, in 1999, a Master of Education degree in Curriculum Studies launches my life in a new direction. I spend the next ten years with the British Columbia Ministry of Education, responsible for implementing graduation program requirements, reviewing report card policies and managing major province-wide projects. Travelling throughout the sixty BC school districts, I work with teachers, principals and superintendents of schools to improve learning outcomes for all BC schoolchildren from Kindergarten through to Grade 12.

In 2009, I change course again. I had long since hit my 10,000 hours[17] of teaching and am now widely considered an expert in student engagement. As an independent educational consultant, I develop and teach courses for Royal Roads University, the University of Victoria, Camosun College and other organizations. Online learning is gaining popularity and my technology skills are in demand. In addition to facilitating workshops and teaching courses, I am frequently invited to

---

[17] A short form of this idea was popularized in Malcolm Gladwell's book, *Outliers*.

deliver keynote addresses at conferences in British Columbia, Australia and other parts of the world.

I also embrace volunteer work, travelling to the poorest, most remote outposts in Kenya, where I provide professional development for teachers and school principals through Education Beyond Borders. This Canadian non-profit organization, dedicated to closing the global education divide, inspires teachers in developing countries, though it runs on a shoestring. The dusty African surroundings are a far cry from the Arctic terrain that I visited years ago, but my mind often wanders back to the time I spent in the North. On the equator, the sun rises and sets at almost exactly the same time every day. You can count on 12 hours of sunshine and 12 hours of darkness regardless of the time of year. How different from my Arctic summer, with 24 hours of continuous daylight for almost four months.

I can't help falling in love with the African children when they look at me with their liquid brown eyes. The trusting faces remind me of the Dene children that I held dear so many years ago. Fleetingly, I wonder: Where are those little Dene boys and girls now? Then my mind returns to the task at hand and we plunge into facilitating a workshop for the teachers.

Educational challenges faced by educators in Kenya can be overwhelming. A Grade 2 teacher has a class of 85 students, most of whom sit on the floor for the lessons. I help her develop strategies for group work. A principal is trying to provide breakfast for students who sometimes faint from hunger. We identify high-calorie foods that can be prepared in large quantities. Another principal, worried about the personal safety of teenaged girls, has opened a girls-only boarding school. Our small team purchases desks and school uniforms for the most destitute schools.

Throughout Africa, the need is great. Resources are so strained that library books are kept under lock and key. Crammed into overcrowded classrooms, students sit tight together, four to a narrow bench. They share textbooks, notebooks and pencils. A use is found for every scrap of paper. Students are required to wear uniforms, a legacy of the British colonial system. The uniforms are then handed down to successively younger family members until the elbows are threadbare and the knees have been patched countless times.

The schools we visit do not employ substitute teachers. When a teacher is ill or absent for any reason, the students are expected to stay in the classroom, unsupervised, and work on their own. African educators work long hours for low pay, sometimes waiting up to three months before receiving their pay cheque. Some are 'untrained teachers' who have graduated from high school and have no post-secondary education at all. Working with the highly motivated Kenyan professionals is rewarding and enlightening. I return to Canada feeling unjustifiably privileged and more than ever determined to support people who are less fortunate.

Contract work with Royal Roads University takes me to China where I work with teachers, principals and school superintendents who plan to improve their education system by learning about western teaching methodologies. My specialization is enhancing student engagement through experiential learning, and participants in the Royal Roads University programs are grateful for my expertise.

The years blur together. I travel to Vietnam, Cambodia, Peru, United Arab Emirates, Turkey and other countries as an educational consultant in both volunteer and paid positions. Nigerian education leaders tell me that my teaching strategies have improved learning outcomes throughout every district where I trained the teachers and administrators. Fascinating people, important decisions, overseas work assignments and brilliant conversations are dimly remembered. Instead, only a few significant events and general impressions make up the fabric of my life during these years. With a family to feed and a career to build, there is no time to think about the past. The Canadian Arctic is a distant memory. Sometimes, deep inside, I catch myself remembering the summer that I spent in the

Sahtu … fishing with friends on Colville Lake, laughing around the bonfire on the shores of Great Bear Lake, and that moment in a little canvas tent, suffused with sunshine, close to my Dene heartthrob. Those dark eyes burning into mine – were there wrinkles at the edges when he smiled?

My secret is safe except for one person – Ethel. No longer a Member of Parliament, my old friend and former classmate has been living in Norman Wells since 2006. When we reminisce from time to time, she still teases me about my long-ago crush on a Dene man. Since so many years have passed and I now enjoy a loving marriage, it's easy for me to laugh about my bygone teenaged infatuation.

The joys of raising a family stretch beyond my wildest dreams. The challenges remind me that we are always learning and growing (2006).

Although I am contributing to school improvement in educational jurisdictions around the world, my longing for social justice remains strong. I still cringe when I think of the human rights abuses suffered by our Indigenous brothers and sisters in Canada. As part of my personal commitment to reconciliation, I make presentations to the First Nations Education Steering Committee (FNESC), British Columbia

Confederation of Parent Advisory Councils (BCCPAC) and other organizations, advocating for Indigenous content in education and Indigenous approaches to student learning.

My forgotten childhood dream of becoming a missionary nun has been replaced with community work, a caring husband, four terrific children and fulfilling employment. Our family maintains spiritual practices, attending church on Sunday, saying grace before meals and praying for our loved ones at day's end. As I approach the end of a successful career, I am happy with my comfortable life – teaching at the university, volunteering overseas, vacationing with the family and generally living a full life. But something is nagging at my conscience and stirring me to action. A deeper sense of purpose is missing. Time for some soul-searching. I begin to reconsider my life's path yet again.

Two seemingly unrelated incidents prompt me to consider whether I am being called to do something different with my God-given skills and knowledge. The year is now 2015 and I am 63 years old. Okay, I still have time on this earth to do something significant, but what? The pivotal moments I am about to describe shaped my decision-making process and determined my destiny over the next five years.

The first happened at a funeral that took place at Holy Cross Roman Catholic Church in Victoria, British Columbia. I wanted to say a quick prayer to my recently deceased friend so I excused myself from the other well-wishers and walked over to the coffin that held the body of Rocky Forest. As I knelt down, I felt a blanket of peace surround me. A sense of great tenderness overwhelmed me. Such deep joy should have been surprising under the circumstances. I could hardly hear the noise, conversations and music in the room because all sounds were somehow muted. This delicious impression lingered as I thanked God for the gift of Rocky's friendship and asked consolation for his widow and family. I wanted to keep praying because of the serene sensation, but it was time for the service to begin, so I blessed myself and stood up.

As I rose, that peaceful feeling melted away and I was back in the church with the crowd of mourners. It all seemed perfectly natural. But, beyond doubt, something had changed within me. Like a glowing ember, the memory of that strange sensation I had felt long ago in the Colville Lake graveyard began to burn again. This time, the peace of mind was accompanied by a troubling awareness that I have a mission to accomplish before, like all mortals, my body succumbs to old age and death. I somehow feel that I am being called back to the Sahtu. The moment passes.

A few months later, an unrelated incident again compels me to contemplate the purpose and direction of my life. It happened in a hotel elevator. An ordinary-looking, middle-aged woman with shoulder-length brown hair got on the elevator and stared at me in surprise. We were the only two people in that small space. Unhesitatingly, this complete stranger declared, "I have to tell you something. You have a powerful presence. I can see a pink aura all around you. You can do something big if you put your mind to it."

That was it. The message was unequivocal. I thanked the woman for her words and exited the elevator on my floor, wondering whether this might be some kind of call to action. I need to take some time to discern the meaning of these messages. Maybe these are signs that I am being summoned back to the Sahtu, back to the people who changed my life irrevocably almost half a century ago. If so, what am I being asked to do? The whispers in my heart are vague and unfocused. I reflect on the seemingly unrelated incidents without arriving at any conclusions.

I am finally convinced to take action after a phone call to Ethel. During our long-overdue chat, my friend tells me that Father Brown ('Mister Brown' since 1971) had passed away on July 11, 2014. I should have expected this news, as he was 94 years old when his soul departed this world. My dad, who was his friend, had died in 1999. Still, the knowledge of Father's

Brown's death startles me. I realize that I have unfinished business from my early adulthood.

"Oh, Ethel! I have a half-written letter to Father Brown on my computer," I sigh.

Ethel responds without hesitating. "You should finish writing that letter and send it to Margaret." There are a few times in my life when I have felt that the decision I make will change the course of my life. This is one of those times. Finish the incomplete letter and mail it off. Then what? Go back up North and ... what? Reconnect with people from long ago ... how?

Ethel's advice inspires me. First, I write the letter and mail it to Margaret. Then, I reach for my diary from 1971. I knew exactly where to find it. How many times had I picked up that tattered notebook and considered tossing it out? Since returning from the North in 1971, I had ruthlessly culled countless sentimental artifacts, dumping old letters, cards, pictures and bank statements. But not my diary from 1971. Somehow, that little journal had made the cut every time. When the time came for me to reread the events from that fateful summer, I didn't even have to think about where to look for my diary. I merely opened the top right-hand drawer of my desk, pulled out a file folder and held the little brown coil notebook in my hands again for the first time in more than four decades.

The worn, wrinkled scribbler held accurate memories of crucial experiences with the Dene in the North when I was still a teenager. With the first glance, I was transported back in time. For all those years, I had tried to ignore that brush with a different world. I had tried to erase the laughter, tried to forget my delight in the people, tried to deny the Dene words and phrases I had learned. My journey of understanding had ended when I left the North in disgrace, fired from my job at Trophy Lodge for drunk and disorderly behaviour.

Now, reading the words I had written as a young woman alone in an extraordinary environment, I finally acknowledge those memories, faded but still intact. What had been an incoherent dream came back into focus. Vivid details of everyday life with the Dene in Colville Lake and Trophy Lodge remind me of that bond we had shared for one brief summer. I relive precious moments that had been obscured by time. Emotions flood over me and the tears flow. Tears of ... what? Gratitude for the experience? Sadness for the destruction of a youthful dream? Anguish for the loss of my first love?

The summer of 1971 had become a core of heartache that I never touched. Thinking about it again made my cheeks burn. Those events represented a miserable failure in my life. But, where I had cringed inside, turning away from the memories, now I am able to embrace those feelings. Where I had dismissed that experience, now I allow myself to recall the images – unending daylight, campfires, canvas tents, sandy beaches, laughter, music and the sheer joy of being young and alive.

The remembrance of that season in my life began to seem like a message from the past. And the author of that past isn't quite the self that I am now. Like a dream remembered, sensations visit themselves upon me in a misty realm of half-reality. Intense, long-repressed feelings surge through me again with a new urgency. Tangled emotions swirl as I remember those golden moments bathed in the glow of the midnight sun.

By the time I finished reading long-forgotten words in the little notebook, I had made a decision to return to the North. I didn't know how I would reconnect with the people I had fallen in love with so many years ago. I didn't know how I would get to Colville Lake. I didn't know what the future held. All I knew for certain was that I was being called back to the North, back to the Dene in the Sahtu. I was willing to surrender to this impulse.

Momentarily, my mind drifts to Trophy Lodge, and I allow myself to wonder ... did Travis share the same memories? Would he recall that moment in the tent when we almost became lovers? What had happened to the young man who had captured my heart so many years ago? Closing my eyes, I remember the sound of his voice, the laughter in his eyes, the way he walked, his tender touch, our innocence and our physical desire. Now that I have opened that window into the past, the memories burn brightly again. Visions of people I once knew dance in my brain. Bewilderingly, my younger self is one of those people.

I think of the men, women and children who were so important to me during those formative months in the Arctic. Reminders of our wordless communication in Colville Lake well up. That mysterious, invisible spirit world summons me, reawakening a long-forgotten yearning to reconnect with the Dene. I think about what might have happened to the boys and girls I had played with every day in that tiny Dene community. Memories of my three faithful companions awaken. Images, scents and tastes sweep over me as I recall wandering dusty trails with giggling children, insects buzzing around us, ravens calling and wood smoke in my nostrils.

Then again … maybe I am just being sentimental. Maybe I have romanticized that chapter of my life. I remember cleaning bloody noses and hugging crying kids, wiping tear-stained faces and washing scraped knees. I remember eating caribou steaks and singing around the campfire ... swarms of black flies ... the smell of fish drying in the sun ... laughter, teasing, playing cards … but maybe events in Colville Lake and Trophy Lodge that summer had actually unfolded differently from the way I remembered. Maybe my imagination had run wild over the intervening years. I had to find out. A wave has swept over me and I feel helpless to resist the force that is taking me back to the Northwest Territories after almost half a century away.

*

The first time I saw a dead body is the moment I realized that every person has a soul. Call it a spirit or whatever you like. In that moment, I knew the truth – human beings are much more than mere flesh and blood and bones. Looking at my father lying in his casket, it was painfully obvious that he was not there. I could see only some kind of human figure; there was no trace of the man who had bounced me on his knee when I was a little girl and walked me down the aisle when I got married. The body that now lay in state had been merely a temporary home for his soul. My dad's soul had left that home, but his influence lives on in my heart.

This notion of a soul surfaces in my mind when I think about Travis. I wonder what causes that frisson between two people? That rare connection when your eyes meet, and you sense a kindred spirit? Why do some people connect strongly with certain individuals and not with others? My father said that moments like this demonstrate the existence of a soul that transcends time and space. His phrasing has stayed with me for more than sixty years. And when I reflect on that formative time in my life, when I was 19 years old and catapulted into a different reality ... that's when my father's words ring more true than ever.

Maybe if someone is meant to be in my life, that soul will gravitate back to mine, no matter how far apart we wander, no matter how much time passes.

*

Decision made, I need some kind of plan. I want to return to the North but have no idea what I will do or how I will reconnect with the Dene people. Mike has provided wise counsel over the years, encouraging me to volunteer overseas and keeping the home fires burning while I travelled on business. When I talk to my life partner about my dilemma, Mike replies simply, "Take a plane to Yellowknife. You will figure out what to do. If you honestly feel the need to go, then go."

My husband's advice is eminently reasonable. He knows me well and I can rely on his advice. Yellowknife is doable. Colville Lake is not. I would need a good reason to go to Colville Lake this time. There are still no all-weather roads to the Sahtu communities, and flying into those remote outposts is prohibitively expensive and time-consuming. Only one airline flies into Colville Lake. Only two flights are scheduled weekly between Yellowknife and Colville Lake. Besides, where would I stay? Who lives there now? Would anyone remember me?

No, visiting Colville Lake is not a viable possibility for many reasons. However, Father Brown had donated thousands of photographs to the Prince of Wales Museum in Yellowknife. To see those images would be worth the cost of the trip. Regularly scheduled flights to Yellowknife mean that I can get to Yellowknife from my home in Victoria in one day. Perhaps I could take my journey back down memory lane by looking through the Yellowknife museum archives. Seeing some familiar faces in those photographs might satisfy my deep yearning to reconnect with the Dene.

Once again, as in 1971, I have no real course of action – no idea what I will do, who I will meet, or where I will stay in Yellowknife. I'm not even sure why I am going. I only know that something is calling me. Blind faith guides me. Perhaps this instinct is merely a reawakening of that long-simmering urge for social justice. Or an end-of-career attempt at closure. After all, the North is where I made my decision to pursue the teaching profession.

At the very least, I owe the Dene people a debt of gratitude for providing some direction to my life. Aside from that, all I know for sure is that a mysterious force compels me. Some might identify it as divine intervention, the whispers of the Holy Spirit or my guardian angel. I only know that I am willing to answer this call yet again.

I still want to speak out against injustice. I still want to be a source of hope in the world. I am still committed to serving Indigenous people. With all four of my children now grown and loving support from my husband, I am free to follow those dreams again. Who knows? This could be my last opportunity to fulfill my teenaged vision of publishing a book about Indigenous heroes.

Walking into the unknown can be daunting, but I feel myself being pulled into another adventure. I guess it's time to pack my bags and head up North again. I'm not afraid of travelling by myself. Fortunately, in 2015, I am armed with credit cards, a cell phone and a suitable wardrobe. But what am I getting myself into this time? I soon learn that what was intended to be a simple visit will turn into something much longer and much more complicated.

11 We've Been Waiting

Certain forces are at work in my life. I seem to be inexplicably drawn to embark on projects that don't seem logical at the time. Like going somewhere for no apparent reason and then finding out I was meant to be there. I have learned to trust that impulse. It happened in 1971 when I first went up North and then again in 2015 when I felt compelled to return to the Sahtu. I really have no idea why I travelled to Yellowknife in 2015. I only know that I had to make an effort to connect with the Sahtu Dene after more than four decades away from those tiny northern communities.

*

Ethel is my only contact in the Northwest Territories, so I phone her with the half-formed hope that we might be able to get together in Yellowknife at some point in time. Nope. She loves her home in Norman Wells and rarely travels south to the big city of Yellowknife. Never mind. I will go alone. This is not the first time I have found myself in uncharted waters without a compass for direction. Embracing the challenge of another adventure, I start planning a tentative itinerary.

I pick my dates out of thin air. Due to my jam-packed teaching schedule, the only time that I can escape from my responsibilities is in mid-September. The Program Associate at Royal Roads University kindly reschedules my classes so that I can leave British Columbia for four days. It will take a day of travel time each way to get to Yellowknife and then home again. I will allow myself three nights and two full days in the capital city of the Northwest Territories.

My husband is a surprising source of information. Mike has been watching a long-running reality television show called *Ice Road Truckers*, which is set in the Yukon, Alaska and the Northwest Territories. He explains that the winter road, also known as the ice road, has changed life in the Arctic. During the coldest six weeks of the year, graders carve roadways over compacted snow, frozen tundra, bare ground and even ice-covered lakes. These temporary roads enable supplies to be brought to remote communities such as Colville Lake, Deline, Fort Good Hope, Tulit'a and Norman Wells, which are otherwise only accessible by air or snowmobile. Driving the winter road can be risky and is not for the faint of heart. The roads are bumpy and unstable, with long empty stretches of snowy tundra between communities. The lack of services or amenities for many miles means that a mechanical breakdown or sudden blizzard can be fatal. Some of the *Ice Road Truckers* episodes set in the Sahtu feature the dangers of driving a heavily loaded truck over the treacherous ice bridge that crosses Great Bear River and Great Bear Lake to Deline. That bridge of pure ice is the only terrestrial access to Deline. The connector consists of seasonal ice frozen to a depth of at least six feet.

Although no all-weather roads connect the Sahtu communities with larger villages and towns, the winter road is an effective way to bring much-needed fuel, freight, goods and machinery to these remote outposts. The winter road transportation route is but one of many changes that I will see in the North.

The Sahtu communities are accessible only by air, except when the winter road is open.

Mike's support strengthens my determination to return to the origin of my dreams, that summer when I made the transition from teenager to adult. With new resolve, I book my flights, reserve a hotel, kiss my husband good-bye and leave Victoria for parts unknown.

There are no non-stop flights from Victoria to Yellowknife, so I have to change planes in Calgary. From Victoria, I take a Boeing 737 to Calgary. The Calgary to Yellowknife leg of the journey takes place on a smaller plane, a Bombardier Q400. From my home in Victoria to the Explorer Hotel in Yellowknife, door to door, takes more than ten hours. By the time I check in at the front desk of the hotel, I am more than ready for a nap. But my exhaustion disappears when I catch sight of a familiar face. "Ethel! What are you doing in Yellowknife?"

Excitedly, my former classmate and I reconnect. We haven't seen each other in many years, but we are immediately laughing and talking as if no time had passed. Both of us feel like teenagers again. Through an extraordinary coincidence, the hotel has assigned us adjacent rooms. Of course! This rendezvous was somehow meant to be. Our joyful reunion lasts well into the night, as we share stories and giggle together.

This remarkable woman fills me in on some of the developments in the Sahtu – my, how times have changed. When Ethel tells me that she is unexpectedly in Yellowknife on business as Chair of the SSI, I ask, "What's the SSI?" My friend laughs and explains that the Sahtu Secretariat Incorporated is an organization that was established to implement the *Sahtu Dene and Metis Comprehensive Land Claim Agreement*. Membership in the SSI is composed of leaders from the five communities in the Sahtu – namely, Colville Lake, Deline, Fort Good Hope, Norman Wells and Tulit'a. These are precisely the same communities that I had visited back in 1971 – another curious coincidence.

The Sahtu region of the Northwest Territories is large in area but small in population. The *Sahtu Dene and Metis Comprehensive Land Claim Agreement* that legally created the Sahtu is known as a modern treaty, a binding agreement between Indigenous inhabitants of the land and the federal and territorial governments. The Sahtu Land Claim Agreement was signed in 1993, more than twenty years after I had visited the five communities. The dots are finally connected – people and places that were important to me as a teenager are now united in the Land Claim. All the loose ends of my summer in the Sahtu are beginning to come together.

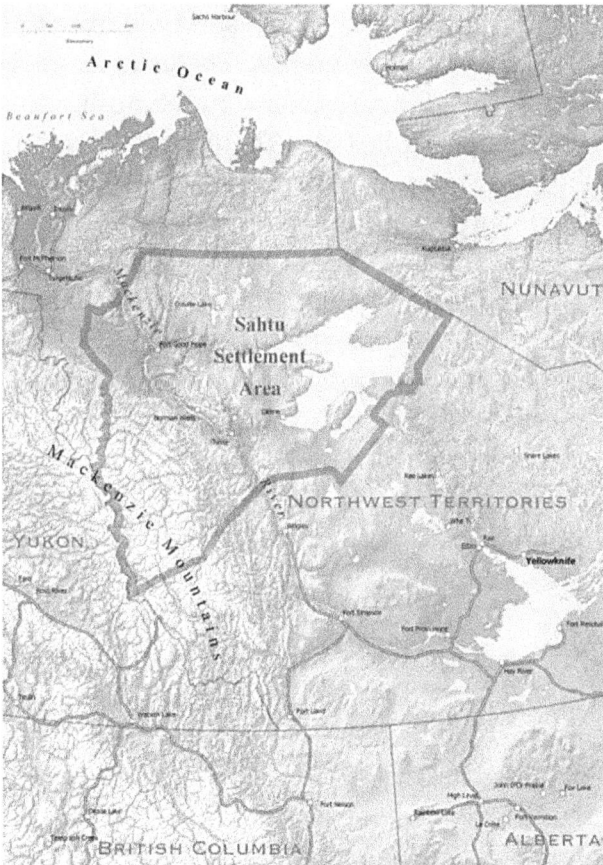

The Sahtu region, established through the *Sahtu Dene and Metis Comprehensive Land Claim Agreement*, encompasses almost 1/3 of Canada's Northwest Territories (map courtesy of *Sahtu Atlas*).

Leaders from throughout the Sahtu have travelled to Yellowknife to meet regarding their common issues. Coincidentally, they are meeting all day tomorrow in the same hotel where I am staying. When Ethel learns that I specialize in teaching experiential learning, student engagement and educational leadership, she insists that I join tomorrow's SSI meeting.

I protest. "What will I say? I don't know these folks!" Ethel's response is simple. "Your knowledge and connections might help my people." Reluctantly, I agree to attend the meeting in the afternoon.

The next morning, I rise early and walk to the Prince of Wales museum to view the archives. At the museum, I find much more than just photographs. The exhibits evoke vivid recollections of my summer sojourn in the bush camp that is now the hamlet of Colville Lake. There are the hides drying in the sun, the sweet faces of the children and the picturesque log cabins that are forever etched in my memory. Hours fly by in a nostalgic haze until I walk back to the hotel for a bite to eat.

After lunch, I am ready to meet the members of the SSI. As I wait outside the boardroom to be called in, I notice the band leaders coming and going. The Dene men, casually clad in jeans, T-shirts and ball caps, glance at me with undisguised curiosity. Some introduce themselves with a friendly smile and handshake before going into the boardroom for their meeting. Ethel is fully occupied keeping the agenda on track and tells me to wait outside the door until an appropriate point on the agenda.

When I am called into the meeting, I sit next to Ethel and scan the room. The assemblage consists of about twenty Indigenous people gathered around a boardroom table. Predominantly male, they sip coffee and chat good-naturedly with each other. Some of the men look vaguely familiar – their facial features remind me of the people I knew 44 years ago.

"Who's your friend, Ethel?" asks a middle-aged man in a plaid shirt and blue jeans.

"I'm just here to listen," I pipe up.

"This is Mary-Anne Neal," Ethel answers. "She is an educator. You'll hear from her a bit later." The meeting continues through agenda items that include environmental protection, mineral exploration, financial statements, justice concerns and educational issues.

I listen intently. When I hear comments about fracking on the Sahtu land, I think, "Royal Roads University has an environmental sustainability program – maybe someone at the university can advise the Dene people about the potential impacts on their land."

Hearing a legal question, I realize that the Justice Institute of BC might provide advice free of charge. When attendees raise complaints about the education system, my mind turns to online learning. Web-based instruction reaches remote and inaccessible areas – maybe my knowledge and skills can help the leaders find a way to address some of the educational challenges faced by the Dene in the Sahtu.

The band leaders in the Sahtu are far more interested in the future than in the past. The residential school legacy is almost irrelevant to their goals; those abuses happened to their parents. These forward thinking men and women have moved beyond colonialism and are working towards self-determination and self-government. I am awed by the magnitude of the issues they face and fascinated by their astute analysis of complex questions.

Finally, one of the band leaders tells Ethel, "We've talked for long enough. It's time for your visitor to tell us a bit about herself." The moment has come. Ethel looks at me.

Deep breath. I stand up. "I've been listening to your concerns, and I think I can connect you with people and programs that can help you find answers to your questions."

Then I list some of the programs and people that might be interested in working with the band leaders to solve some of the challenges in their communities.

"But who are you?" asks a man sitting near the door.

All eyes are on me. I pause. It is not going to be easy for me to speak the truth out loud about my long-ago visit to Colville Lake. Maybe I should just explain my professional credentials and leave it at that. But … these people have the right to know a bit about my personal reasons for being in Yellowknife. Unsure how to describe the inexplicable motivations behind my presence, I hesitate, then look into the eyes of the Dene leaders.

"Well, I visited Colville Lake one summer a long time ago," I begin. "1971, to be exact. I stayed with Father Brown just before he got married to Margaret Steen. While I was there, I helped him run the fishing lodge. I really loved playing with the kids in Colville, and I tried to learn a bit of the language."

A peculiar look comes over some faces, but I plow ahead.

"I admire the Dene for many reasons. It is because of that summer that I became a teacher. So I feel like I owe the people of the Sahtu some credit for my career as an educator."

When I stop talking, I sense a different kind of silence in the room. The faces of the people looking at me have changed. I can't read their expressions. No one speaks.

Then a man with a shock of thick black hair sitting directly across from me breaks the silence. "We know who you are."

"How could you possibly know who I am??!!"

"Our parents and grandparents told us about you. You are the white girl who spent a summer in Colville Lake."

A hand goes up: "I remember you. I'm Joseph." Another hand: "I'm Wilbert."

I gasp. "Whaaat? You are the little boys who played ball with me in Colville Lake so long ago! You mean … you actually remember me?"

"The Elders told us that you would return. We've been waiting for you. We need your help now more than ever."

And then the words that I didn't realize I had been waiting for: "When can you come back?"

After the meeting with the Sahtu band leaders in Yellowknife, memories that had been painful suddenly became cherished. Knowing that the Dene remembered those moments and retold them to their children and grandchildren renews my age-old commitment to honour Indigenous voices. The bonds we had forged together under the blaze of the midnight sun were stronger than I ever suspected.

The shame that I felt almost half a century ago is now bittersweet. The unthinkable – being dismissed from a job – is just a small part of my life story now, at age 63. I don't know what the future holds, but the Dene of the Sahtu will be part of it.

*

The meeting is over. SSI representatives are leaving the boardroom. Ethel and I are chatting quietly when one of the meeting participants, a stranger to me, comes over to us. I look up and our eyes lock. The unmistakable gleam in those dark brown eyes, the calm smile ... could this spare, grey-haired fellow possibly be Travis? The handsome Dene man just looks at me steadily and holds out his hand. In his chiseled face I see a glimmer of the youth I had known more than four decades ago. That summer romance was not just a dream. Without words, I recognize the boy within the man. My heart skips a beat, and I can't stop smiling. Taking Travis' outstretched hand, I whisper, "So you are real."

Now a respected band councilor, Travis has come to the annual SSI meeting as a representative of Deline to discuss issues held in common by the five communities. This Dene man is dedicated to his community and has travelled throughout Canada for more than twenty years, advocating for self-government on behalf of his people. Travis has been happily married for forty years and is rightly proud of the six children he and his wife have raised. I chuckle to myself, remembering that I had wanted to have eight children. Between us, we now have ten children!

Ethel laughs as Travis and I stumble over our words in an effort to restore that lost connection. Almost half a century ago, we had been teenagers falling in love. Now our lives have come full circle. A common desire to support the Sahtu Dene people has brought us together again. Travis and I agree to catch up on each other's lives over dinner that night.

I am a grandmother, but I feel like a teenager again – excited and nervous to finally reconnect with the first man I had ever loved. This evening will be just a friendly chat to find out what has happened over all those years, but … what will I wear? Will we run out of topics for conversation? We have found each other again ... what happens now?

Sitting in the hotel restaurant that night, Travis and I immediately feel comfortable together and relax into easy conversation. Our lives have unfolded very differently during the intervening years. Surprisingly, both of us have clung to the memory of that sun-drenched summer at Trophy Lodge. We had kept a spark of hope alive that we might someday reconnect, and now we are eager to reminisce. Travis wants to tell me the whole story from his point of view.

"Mary-Anne," he says quietly. "I still remember when you left Trophy Lodge in 1971. After making lunch on shore, I had a funny feeling, so I brought my guest back to the lodge early. When I walked into that tent cabin where the guides were staying, there was a note sitting on my table. The note said that you were going back to Edmonton. I knew the plane was still at the float dock, so I jumped into my boat and headed over to the float plane. As I got close to the float dock, I saw the plane was taxiing away. I gunned the motor and roared behind it, but I couldn't catch the plane before it started to lift off. Then I was so mad I just sat in my boat, raging helplessly as that float plane took you away from me."

Tears spring to my eyes and dinner is forgotten as Travis' words rekindle buried memories. "That's when I was crying my eyes out, too," I manage to choke out over the lump in my throat.

So I hadn't imagined it all. I can trust my memory. For one brief summer, this man and I had shared the beginnings of a

140

sweet, innocent love. My life would have been so different if only I hadn't been sent away from the North and the youth who had captured my heart. Our conversation brings clarity to half-remembered moments.

Travis recollects events of that summer in much greater detail than I do. He treasured the little love notes that I had tucked into his lunch pail for him to find when he fried up fish for the shore lunches with his guests. He can call up the songs he strummed on his guitar while I sang along. He vividly remembers that bittersweet afternoon in the tent when we almost became lovers.

Most importantly to me, Travis recalls every minute of that fateful night when I was fired from my job at the fishing lodge. I want to know what happened after I blacked out. Travis tells me that he had noticed Don, manager of the guides, hanging around our campfire that fateful night. For some reason, Don was watching me and Travis closely. Maybe the guide manager had seen us go off alone together that afternoon. Travis and I had been holding hands a lot around the camp; it was no longer a secret that we liked each other.

At one point that night, Travis stopped playing his guitar and bent over to kiss me. As he did so, he noticed that Don was staring at us scornfully. Travis believes that Don did not want a Dene guide and a white girl to be together. Don must have told Lynn, the girls' manager, that our budding romance needed to be broken up.

Oh! That explains why Lynn called me a tramp. Finally the pieces of the puzzle are fitting together and I begin to make sense of my sudden dismissal from the lodge. In the management view, a white girl had no place falling in love with a Dene man. Travis and I had broken that unwritten rule. I had been punished, not so much for drunkenness, but for daring to fall in love with a non-white. After all those years, I am beginning to understand the racism that tore me from Travis' arms. Listening to Travis retell our story, I feel the pain again and recall the numbness that set in after a few months apart. Our young love had been ended by others who saw only our differences.

Travis' dark brown eyes betray only a hint of regret. "That experience is one I have never forgotten." He speaks so softly I can hardly hear him. "I used to go up on the roof of my cabin and look at the stars in the night sky. I would lie on my back, looking at the moon and thinking, 'She is out there somewhere, under the same moon that I am looking at right now.' Because of you, I never went back to Trophy Lodge."

The polite, gentle man sitting across from me looks down, clears his throat and with a shrug says, "You sent me a letter with a black-and-white picture of you. For more than thirty years, I kept that photo with me wherever I went. On my way to Ottawa a few years ago, my luggage went missing, along with your picture and the letter. But I kept you in my heart."

I am surprisingly touched that Travis had treasured the letter that I sealed with a kiss almost half a century ago. Mailing back a response would have been far too complicated and challenging for him back then. Fort Franklin might as well have been Mars in terms of communication. News from the outside world took months to reach that remote community. Travis' writing skills were limited, and he had no way to buy a postage stamp, let alone mail a letter. Despite these barriers, both of us had kept a spark of hope alive that we might someday be reunited.

Travis continues, "The day after you left, a float plane arrived at Trophy Lodge from Colville Lake. Somebody named Alouie had chartered it. He was looking for you. Is that someone you know?"

"Oh my goodness! Alouie went to Trophy Lodge looking for me? Why would he do that? Yes, he was my friend in Colville Lake. We went fishing together. He played guitar for me. But never mind that. Tell me about your life now."

"Today I'm busy helping my people. I've been sober for the last 24 years. Life is great. It's even better now, as you and

I are connected again." And with that shy smile, "Maybe we could be friends for life."

Listening to Travis again after more than four decades, I recognize the same humble, good-natured individual that I once knew. The man sitting across from me remembers the tiny silver cross I wore so long ago. Aside from my wedding rings, the cross is still the only jewelry I wear. Travis notices it around my neck tonight. I can almost feel his gentle touch again and I remember his long-ago advice that the cross will protect me. It has protected me this far.

I can't help noticing Travis' brown hands on the white restaurant tablecloth. The hands that I had admired fifty years ago are still strong and unwrinkled, perhaps nurtured by a lifelong diet of clean lake trout with its high Omega 3 content.

Love for the Dene of the Sahtu has brought Travis and me together again even when life kept us apart. Like two rivers that flow together briefly, are separated by a large island and then stream together again, Travis and I have been reunited through a confluence of events. A current based on our shared hopes and dreams carries us along. The coincidences that have brought us together indicate that we are travelling in the right direction. Different life journeys have brought us to the same destination.

When we compare notes from our lives, Travis and I learn that we still share the same values of tolerance, respect and service to others. Both of us are devoted to our families, cherishing our spouses, children and grandchildren. In 1985, when I was a single mom struggling to raise two small children, Travis was building a log house for himself, his wife and their six children. In 1999, when I went back to university to earn a Master of Education degree, Travis was travelling to Ottawa negotiating self-government for Deline. Though our lives have followed different paths, we effortlessly find common ground regardless of the topic.

I tell Travis that I have a pink aura and he says he has been told the same. We search the term on the internet and learn that pink aura people are loving and give generously of their time. They are romantic and stay faithful to their soulmates. Pink aura individuals hate injustice, poverty and conflict. They strive to make the world a better place and make personal sacrifices in pursuit of this ideal. Laughing, we agree wholeheartedly with the description. We will remain loyal to our spouses while maintaining a friendship. Our earnest discussions last well into the night, and we leave each other promising to keep in touch.

12   Understanding the Dene

To everything there is a season
and a time to every purpose.

Ecclesiastes 3 (*The Holy Bible*)

The long flights back to Victoria the next day give me ample time for reflection. With Travis' revelations and the clarity of hindsight, I now recognize the undercurrent of racism that bubbled beneath the surface of the group camaraderie at Trophy Lodge – discrimination against the Dene that I had somehow overlooked. I begin to wonder again if there might be some way that I can now show others the Dene as I see them – heroic, humble, funny, strong, sensitive, loyal, spiritual leaders.

I return to Victoria brimming with enthusiasm. There are so many ways that people in the south can support our fellow Canadians in the North. Over the next few months, every discussion with friends, neighbours, family members and colleagues inevitably turns to the Dene of the Sahtu. My conversation partners are intrigued, but my animated statements are met with quizzical looks. *Where is the Sahtu? What do you mean by 'Dene'? How do you pronounce that word? Why would anyone want to live that far north?* Clearly, some education is needed. I patiently explain what I know to anyone who will listen.

The word *Dene* means 'people.' The Dene refer to the land they inhabit in the North as *Denendeh*, which means 'the Creator's spirit flows through this land' or 'Land of the People.' Measured in terms of population and land area, the Dene are the largest group of Indigenous people in North America. Until the arrival of Europeans, more than eighty large tribes of Dene roamed freely throughout a vast territory, from what is now known as Alaska all the way through Canada to Mexico, totaling more than 1.16 million square kilometres or 450,000 square miles. The Navajo of the southern United States of America call themselves *Dine* (people) and share a common language with the Dene farther north.

Some say that the Dene have occupied the northern geographic region for 10,000 years. The Dene of the Sahtu survive and thrive in one of the harshest climates on our planet. Extreme temperatures and long months of darkness are accepted as part of the natural rhythm. The collective Dene identity is bound up with the open space and natural resources of their homeland. Survival in these severe conditions depends on specialized skills, an understanding of nature's elements and the ability to solve problems creatively. Scientists who study physiology tell us that a deep knowledge of the land and weather is actually embedded in Dene genes.

Until the 1700s, Europeans were unknown to the Dene in the Northwest Territories. For the most part, non-Indigenous people stayed close to the 49th parallel, where the climate is more forgiving, the food more plentiful and the land richer for agriculture. When Alexander Mackenzie travelled north to the Arctic Ocean in 1786, he opened the fur trade in the Mackenzie Valley and surrounding area. Early non-Dene fur traders, hunters, trappers and explorers depended on the Dene for survival. Over the next 200 years, the relationship between the original inhabitants of the North and outsiders became increasingly more complicated, leading to today's complex social, educational, political and environmental challenges.

During the months that follow my visit to Yellowknife, Travis and I communicate regularly, catching up on significant events of his life in Deline and my life in Victoria. We discover that we are equally dedicated to honouring Dene Elders and inspiring Dene youth. Our conversations reveal gripping details of Travis' Indigenous history and identity. As in 1971, I am fascinated with the lifestyle he describes and his stories of growing up in the bush.

Communication in 2015 is instantaneous, a sharp contrast to our vain reliance on the non-existent postal service in 1971.

Now we talk on the phone, video chat, text message and send each other pictures – him butchering a moose or me picking strawberries in my garden. We laugh companionably, those youthful stirrings of romantic love replaced by a comfortable camaraderie tinged with nostalgia and hope for the future.

Like everyone in the Sahtu communities, Travis and his family members still fish almost every day, summer and winter. Moose and caribou form a large part of their diet. Much of my friend's time is spent cleaning and drying fish, butchering caribou and preparing hides for making drums. He has become a gifted artist and photographer. Along with friends and family, Travis participates in community meetings, feasts, festivals and drum dances. Deline's annual Spiritual Gathering in mid-August is a highlight of the year for Travis, his extended family and many people throughout in the Sahtu. Held to commemorate the Deline prophets and also to celebrate the Feast of the Assumption of the Blessed Virgin Mary[18] on August 15, the Spiritual Gathering draws people from all five Sahtu communities and beyond.

My old friend still plays the guitar almost every day. Now his wife, daughters and granddaughters sing along with him. He remains devoted to his older brother and his community. Rooted in the land, Travis keeps cultural practices alive and speaks the Dene language with friends and family members. His priority nowadays is teaching his children and grandchildren the knowledge and skills required to live off the land – hunting, fishing, trapping and camping in the bush and snow. A self-appointed keeper of Dene oral history, he listens to audio and video recordings of the Elders over and over until he has memorized every detail.

I shake my head at the contrast between our lives. My husband and I hired a contractor to build our home in Victoria in 2015. We designed the structure and the house was

---

[18] A Christian feast day honouring the day that the body of the Virgin Mary was assumed into heaven after her death.

constructed by workers. On the other hand, Travis designed and built his log home entirely by himself in 1985. This feat required hauling 240 logs from the boreal forest around Great Bear Lake. He used a chainsaw to fell the trees, skin the branches and cut the tree trunks to the correct length. Then he transported the logs to Deline by snowmobile and carefully installed them in a building of his own design. This hard-working craftsman skillfully completed all the drywall, painting, plumbing and electrical work himself.

Travis still plays guitar daily.

Ever the philosopher, Travis believes that all human beings have powers given to us by the Creator. We don't always use our powers but all things are possible if we just tap into that energy source as the Dene ancestors were able to do eons ago. Travis also trusts that everything happens for a reason. Good or bad, we must make the most of every situation.

Limited formal schooling does not prevent Travis from reading widely to educate himself in local and global issues such as climate change, the justice system, history, domestic violence, addiction and politics. This thoughtful man is a critical thinker. He reflects on what he learns and asks insightful questions, rereading the literature many times over to ensure that he fully understands the writer's perspective.

Travis describes the political landscape in Canada as a series of imaginary borders and invisible structures that separate people. His vision is for people to live, share, create and evolve together. "We are all members of the human race," he explains patiently. "That's what *Dene* means. We are all *Dene*, all human."

A discussion of racism leads Travis to identify the primary cause of our separation 44 years ago. Sharing our thoughts over the phone, Travis and I begin to understand that our young love had been betrayed by the fears of a generation that did not understand our common humanity. Finally, I recognize that our nascent union had been severed due to subtle forms of racial bias. After the initial pain of those memories, speaking the truth out loud about our long-ago summer love is somehow freeing.

When Travis reads my diary from 1971, he encourages me to tell our story so that other people will understand the truth about prejudice against Indigenous men and women. He speaks with integrity, and his message is clear: All people are created equal. It's wrong to divide people based on skin colour, culture or any other arbitrary standard. I sense a strong moral obligation behind this man's suggestion that the story of our unrequited love could motivate people to look beyond race and colour. First, I need to fully understand what happened from his perspective.

Together, Travis and I recreate some of the events that took place at Trophy Lodge. Our conversations slowly reveal the hidden discrimination that had pervaded our camp. For some reason, I had been blind to the ways in which the Dene guides were often excluded from activities and interactions with the white guides. Now, with a shock, I recall the subtle

149

power plays and undercurrent of animosity between the Dene and non-Dene. The manager was correct in acknowledging the existence of racism. Casting me out of the camp was a way to punish me and Travis for daring to kiss in public. But the power imbalance between the Indigenous and non-Indigenous staff ran deeper than our budding romance.

Perhaps because I moved easily between groups of white and Dene, I had been oblivious to the many small ways in which the Dene were slighted by the non-Dene. This does not excuse my behaviour. I had noticed some kind of invisible barrier but had joined in the laughter at discriminatory comments thinly disguised as jokes. Words that I had brushed aside as inconsequential I now realize were painfully derogatory. I had ignored my white friends' use of terms such as 'squaws' and 'bucks' to refer to the Dene. No one challenged the veiled remarks that barely concealed contempt for Indigenous people. When I reflect now on my silence, I feel that perhaps I was somewhat complicit in the casual indignities that had systematically diminished the social standing of the Dene guides in our camp. This growing awareness saddens me now.

My affinity for the Dene had rendered me heedless of the inequities that existed in our staff team. From my lived experience and discussions with Travis about those elusive memories, I now begin to understand some of the complex nuances of the employee relationships at the fishing lodge. A veneer of camaraderie had masked deep unconscious bias on the part of my non-Dene colleagues. Behind their joking lay ignorance of the true Indigenous spirit. But where was my voice defending my Indigenous friends? I vow never again to remain silent.

Travis and I decide that we can begin an honest, national conversation about racism by sharing our personal experience with a larger audience. Combatting subtle forms of prejudice requires a change of heart in people who might not even recognize racism within themselves. Maybe there is something

Travis and I can do to demonstrate the strength and resilience of the Dene people. Before lasting change can happen, others must first become aware of their own subconscious bias. Then they need to comprehend the enormous negative impact that their race-based beliefs and actions have on the souls of those around them. Our story of innocent love divided by racial prejudice could be the first step in creating awareness of underlying, perhaps unwitting prejudice. With knowledge comes understanding. Then, possibly, acceptance. A movie about our unrequited romance would touch people's hearts. Maybe we could write a book? A song? A poem? We agree that, at the very least, we will consistently model forgiveness and tolerance as we go about life with our families and communities.

With Travis as teacher, I begin to understand racism through Dene eyes. Travis takes a keen interest in my career and I rely on his advice regarding all things Dene. True to his word, he supports my efforts to honour the Dene people in film, on social media and in print. I send letters to newspaper editors and encourage filmmakers to document the Dene history and culture. We must do whatever we can to eliminate race-based discrimination.

Travis reminds me of the Deline prophets he had told me about so long ago. Then he tells me that we are all part of the prophecy. This revelation, too, makes sense. No wonder I feel such a strong moral obligation to the Dene. If I am part of the larger context of the prophecy, this explains why I feel compelled to talk about the Dene people, why every conversation somehow turns to the North, and why I am willing to give up other projects to work on this vague, formless notion of returning to the Dene in the North. Could it be true that I am fulfilling the Deline prophecy? Deep down, I don't feel like I am acting of my own volition. Instead, I feel like I am an instrument or a channel for a larger master plan.

Travis' explanation of the Deline prophecies aligns with my Christian beliefs. Faith in a higher power has carried me this far in life, and his reasoning penetrates the veil of mystery surrounding my memories of the summer of 1971. I am reminded of my late father's words that we are only passing through this world for a short time; we must invest our time on earth wisely.

According to Travis, my dismissal from Trophy Lodge was not accidental. It might have been some kind of divine intervention required to achieve a higher goal. Unquestionably, I never would have left the North voluntarily. I accept this premise because clearly Travis and I were not meant to be together. Fine, but we have been reunited for a reason. We just have to discover what we are being called to do.

The series of coincidences that have led to our reunion after so many years apart are nothing short of remarkable. What Carl Jung referred to as *synchronicity* might explain the events that have transpired to place me at the centre of a network of connections among the Dene in the Sahtu. Synchronicity is a term coined by Carl Jung to describe meaningful coincidences that cannot be explained by logic. My life has been characterized by innumerable coincidental occurrences such as the ones described in this book. As my father, the writer, often said, "Truth is stranger than fiction."

Some will say the curious circumstances in anyone's life are a result of mere luck or chance, fortune or misfortune. Regardless of whether the events I experienced were predestined, my life journey has shifted again, this time in a new, more inspiring direction. I ask the Holy Spirit to open my eyes and guide me in discerning the next steps. Maybe Travis and I are destined to be part of something greater than we can imagine.

Everyone needs a sense of purpose and I am no exception. It's possible that the time is finally right for me and Travis to honour the Sahtu Dene people somehow. It's a vague, unformed vision and again I muse about what the final product might look like. A web site? An opera? Travis encourages me to compose music and poetry that might capture the loss we felt in our youth. My attempts to comply with his request are laughable.

My thoughts daily turn to the people of Colville Lake. Maybe there is some way that I can reconnect with those peaceful, warm-hearted men, women, teens and children that I knew so long ago. Finding my old friends again would be a dream come true. Might be too much to ask. Still, I wonder if the skills and knowledge I have acquired over the past half century might benefit the welcoming people who unwittingly gave direction to my adolescent life. Now that I have one foot in the Sahtu, perhaps I can somehow find my way back to the small Dene community where my journey of understanding began.

Then comes the phone call that transforms my life yet again. David Codzi is the President of Ayoni Keh Land Corporation in Colville Lake. The son of my old friend, Jean-Marie Oudzi, David was present at the SSI meeting in September and he has been quietly speculating whether my skills and knowledge might support educational improvement in the Sahtu. This astute young man has a keen intellect. He wants to see first-hand my strategies for experiential learning, and he also intends to determine the possibility of bringing distance learning to the Sahtu. David will come to Victoria if I am available to meet with him. Yes, of course – delighted to get together!

When David and his brother-in-law, Fred John Barnaby, visit me on Vancouver Island in January, 2016, we tour Royal Roads University and the University of Victoria. I demonstrate online learning and student engagement methods so he can determine whether this kind of expertise might benefit youth in the Sahtu. After three intense days discussing the education system and other challenges faced by remote Indigenous communities in the far North, David begins to seem like part of the family. After all, the young man is only two years older than my oldest son.

David Codzi and Fred John Barnaby toured Royal Roads University with me in January, 2016.

During our final dinner together, David tells me that his mother remembers me very well. She told her son, "*Sayday Marie* has a good heart. You can trust her." Then David invites me to conduct an assessment of the education system in Colville Lake and Fort Good Hope. As a guest of the band leaders, my travel expenses and a modest stipend will be paid. I accept his offer without hesitation, knowing that another adventure awaits.

Hooray! After 45 years away from my Dene friends, I'm going back to the Sahtu!

13   Winds of Change

Be not afraid. Just believe.

Mark 5:36 (*The Holy Bible*)

From the snow-capped Mackenzie Mountain peaks west of Norman Wells, then north of Colville Lake to the grassy tundra, east beyond the vast expanse of Great Bear Lake, then south and west back to the mountains ... the Sahtu region stretches across almost one-third of Canada's Northwest Territories, encompassing five distinct communities, countless lakes, immense mountain ranges, boreal forests, vast wetlands, thick bush and majestic rivers. Often called 'the beating heart of the North,' the Sahtu is home to 15 diverse ecosystems as well as to strong, resilient people who have inhabited their homeland for many thousands of years. Known as the Dene, the People, these denizens of the North roamed freely across the tundra, through the boreal forest and over the frozen lakes. In this bleak climate, they hunted, fished, sang, drummed, told stories, raised families, gathered in small communities and travelled long distances, always living close to the land.

*

Almost half a century after my teenaged adventure in the far North, I am finally on my way to reunite with the Dene of Colville Lake. Instead of squeezing into Father Brown's Cessna 180, I am a passenger in a Cessna Caravan flown by North-Wright Airways. Yes, in 2016, there are daily scheduled passenger flights to the tiny community that was accessible only by private aircraft in 1971. Yesterday, I flew from Yellowknife to Norman Wells on a Beechcraft 1900. After overnighting in Norman Wells, today I have boarded an even smaller aircraft, the Cessna Caravan, to fly into Fort Good Hope and then on to my final destination, the hamlet of Colville Lake.

Travelling to Colville Lake in 2016 is an entirely different experience from my excursion in 1971. Instead of begging rides with sympathetic pilots, this time I reserve flights on commercial airlines. First, I fly from Victoria, British Columbia, to Calgary, Alberta. In Calgary, I change planes and fly to Yellowknife, Northwest Territories. Beginning in Yellowknife, I retrace my teenaged footsteps. I overnight in Yellowknife, then find my way to a small hangar where I catch a North-Wright Airways flight to Norman Wells. Another overnight in Norman Wells. A smaller plane to Fort Good Hope. And finally, three days after leaving home, I fly on to Colville Lake. Even in 2016, travel to Colville Lake is time-consuming and expensive. Maybe that's why some say it is still the most remote settlement in North America.

On this trip, I have a few hours of free time to look around Yellowknife. Not surprisingly, the northern city is no longer the one-street town I had toured in 1971. With almost 20,000 people, it is by far the largest community in the Northwest Territories, as well as the economic hub and capital city. The name is derived from a local Dene tribe, the Yellowknives Dene First Nation, whose members carried copper knives when the first fur traders arrived in the 1800s.

Where Yellowknife had limited accommodation in 1971, the city now boasts a hotel and a couple of motels, along with a variety of restaurants and bars, even a movie theatre. In addition to franchise restaurants such as A&W and MacDonald's, I spot a sushi café, Vietnamese noodle house, bistro and quaint specialty eateries. Old Town is still charming, though the multi-coloured shacks have been replaced with bungalows, shops and metal warehouses. My room at the Explorer Hotel is very comfortable and the hotel restaurant features fine dining with northern flavours.

I am surprised to see Asian tourists on the streets and in the hotel. From November until April, travellers from Japan and China flock to Yellowknife for spectacular views of the Northern Lights (also known as the *Aurora Borealis*) under the night sky. Local entrepreneurs shuttle the sightseers to vantage points where teepees are set up for the comfort of their guests.

But I have no time for the Northern Lights and no desire to go out for dinner. I have spent the last three weeks researching the education system in the Northwest Territories. I have developed PowerPoint presentations, survey questions and documents that will help inform my assessment of the education system in the Sahtu. My evening in Yellowknife is spent poring over details and trying to determine where I will go and who might be available to meet with me.

I take a cab to the airport the next day, leaving lots of time for my flight to Norman Wells. There, I meet the first of many transportation challenges. At the main Yellowknife airport terminal, I search in vain for a North-Wright Airways ticket agent. I begin by asking the Air Canada and WestJet staff where I might find the North-Wright flights. No one at the main terminal has heard of this obscure airline. After some digging, I find a person who explains that I will have to head back down the main road to the south end of the runway. There I would find a small building that serves as the North-Wright reception area. Thinking that my destination can't be farther than a couple of blocks, I set off on foot. But finding the tucked-away hangar is not as straightforward as I had hoped. The farther I walk, pulling my wheeled luggage behind me on the icy road, the more anxious I become. Where in heaven's name is North-Wright Air?

A pickup truck passes me, then slows down and pulls over. Two scruffy young men dressed in coveralls and ball caps take pity on me and offer to help me find the elusive North-Wright Airways terminal. We drive down a few different roads until we find a series of blue and gray buildings at the other end of the airport. An inconspicuous sign indicates that we are at the right place. Seems like visitors to the Sahtu are few and far between. I thank the young men from the bottom of my heart, grab my suitcase, wave goodbye and open the door of the small, square building.

The North-Wright waiting room holds about twenty chairs, a green counter and a weigh scale. A few boxes are piled against the wall behind the desk. A prominent sign warns passengers to wear appropriate winter clothing or they will be denied boarding. Behind the counter, a young man with shaggy dark hair, brown eyes and a friendly smile checks my name on a list. He politely asks me to put my luggage on the weigh scale. Next, he weighs my carry-on and handbag. Finally, my young friend says, "Okay. Your turn. Step on the scale, please." I guess these little planes have to account for every pound of weight.

Travellers to the Sahtu are not subjected to security checks because the flights are all internal, within the Northwest Territories. There are no lineups, just a few people heading back to their home communities from the big city in the south. Yes, although Yellowknife is north of the sixtieth parallel, it is hundreds of miles south of the Sahtu. Now that I have checked in with the ticket agent, I relax with the *News of the North* newspaper until it's time to board our Beechcraft 1900. Five other passengers will accompany me on our flight to Norman Wells today. All are Indigenous and all are male. Some things clearly have not changed in 45 years. Aside from a few curious glances at me, my fellow travellers are busy on their cell phones or saying farewell to their companions.

A youthful, fresh-faced pilot with a blonde brush cut calls out a five-minute warning as a reminder for passengers to use the washroom before boarding the plane. Boarding passes are unnecessary. Sit wherever you like. There are no overhead bins in the little aircraft, no onboard bathroom facilities and certainly no snacks provided to passengers. Once we are safely settled on board, the captain of our aircraft introduces himself as Bruce and his co-pilot as Xander. Xander also welcomes us and delivers a short safety briefing. It's okay to bring non-alcoholic drinks on the plane and to use our cell phones while we still have reception. The Beechcraft 1900 has room for 11 passengers and nearly a ton of freight. Today, six of us are flying to Norman Wells with a full cargo load.

As the plane rises into the sky, I watch a surreal landscape unfold below. Like blotches of white paint on a gray canvas, the frozen lakes, rivers, tundra, marsh and muskeg are all interconnected. The ice-covered scene as far as the eye can see reminds me of modern art, but the image unfolding below is more entrancing than any painting because the panorama is ever-changing. Even the drone of the engines can't lull me to sleep when the scenery is so fascinating. The long flight at a low altitude gives me plenty of time to absorb the sight. Undulating rivers and creeks, random patches of muskeg and endless, snow-covered boreal forest – the wild, natural beauty takes my breath away.

The landscape appears desolate and unforgiving from above, but it is a living universe for the Dene who draw their lives from its substance. Treeless stretches of tundra and lake-studded, forested regions provide sustenance for the people who have lived in this harsh climate for millennia. More of the land mass in the North is covered by lakes, swamps, streams and rivers than almost any other land surface in the world.

Staring out the icy window, I also see a maze of cut lines stretching to the horizon in every direction. These are straight, ten-foot-wide lines cut through the forest and tundra, usually by the energy industry. Where in 1971 there was only boreal forest and tundra, now I see evidence of innumerable man-made swaths slicing through the wilderness. Extraction companies have been busy. As I close my eyes, I feel a chill of apprehension ... what other changes await me in the Sahtu?

Cut lines such as these crisscross the Arctic.

In Norman Wells, Ethel greets me with hugs and a torrent of information about the people, activities, history and culture of her beloved homeland. My old friend tours me around the scenic little town and I am enchanted with the slanting rays of sunlight, hoar-covered trees and neatly planned streets. How had I managed to forget the charm of this picturesque locale?

The majestic Mackenzie Mountain range rises in the distance beyond the huge frozen expanse of the Mackenzie River. Looking across the valley, I see the smaller Franklin and Richardson mountains, shrouded in birch and spruce. Although there are only about four hours of daylight in January, a full six hours of twilight tint the sky with delicate swirls of pink, orange and yellow that slowly fade to blue and purple. The dark sky is the perfect backdrop for the moon, the stars and the incomparable Northern Lights.

Amid the natural beauty I notice something very odd. I don't recall seeing islands in the Mackenzie River near Norman Wells when I stayed there 45 years ago. And what are all those man-made contraptions sticking up out of the strange-looking islands? Ethel informs me that six islands were built by Esso Resources Canada in 1984 as a way to efficiently extract oil from a natural underground formation called an oil reservoir below the river. I cannot imagine the magnitude of

160

the environmental impact caused by these man-made islands on the river's fragile ecosystem. And what about the cost of remediation when the oil field is no longer producing? According to Ethel, the company employs very few northern workers, preferring to bring in trained staff from the south. Has oil extraction benefited the Dene who have inhabited the land for countless millennia? Or has it caused problems for the First People of the Mackenzie Valley? Our intense discussions lead me to conclude that the economic benefits of development have accrued elsewhere. I fall asleep that night wondering if the Dene's innate connection with the land has suffered due to mining and mineral exploration.

After a night at the Sahtu Dene Inn, I am back at the Norman Wells airport early the next morning. My body weight is already on file at North-Wright Airways, so only the baggage needs to go on the scale. Soon I follow Louis, our twenty-something pilot, out on to the tarmac and clamber aboard the Cessna Caravan that will take me and two other passengers north to Fort Good Hope, also known as the Charter Community of K'Asho Got'ine (where the rapids are). After a quick stop in the little hamlet, we will carry on beyond the Arctic Circle, northeast to Colville Lake.

The interior of the little Cessna Caravan shows evidence of heavy usage – frayed upholstery, worn armrests, fabric rubbed shiny from many bodies, grease stains on the seats. The letters have long ago rubbed off the EXIT sign on the door. A hard piece of metal pokes out of my armchair cover. It takes me a few minutes to buckle up because the three-point harness is initially a mystery. The seatbelt straps go over the chest and also around the waist. We don't need a co-pilot for this little plane, but the space where one would sit is useful for storage. The seat next to the pilot is piled high with documents, work gloves, manifest, a jacket, a multi-pouch zippered bag, DayGlo vest, file folder, maps and even a couple of books – *Hartzell Propeller Owner's Manual* and the *DGLC Pilot's Operating*

Handbook. Now that I am safely settled in my seat, I gaze out grimy windows blooming with frost.

Great view from the co-pilot's seat when travelling between the small communities.

Our pilot flies low, following the mighty Mackenzie River northwest for 145 kilometres. I am awed by the magnificent cliffs, carved by the river's current millennia ago and imposing even from great distances. Twenty minutes later, we land at Fort Good Hope, a town of about 500 people overlooking the Mackenzie. The other two passengers disembark, some cargo and luggage is offloaded, and a middle-aged man bound for Colville Lake boards the plane. The only other passenger looks vaguely familiar. Something about the shaggy hair and square jaw reminds me of … it's Edward Oudzi! Laughter and handshakes when we recognize each other. I haven't reached Colville Lake yet and already my past is catching up to me. It has been almost three full days since I left my home in Victoria; the final leg of my convoluted journey is at hand.

162

From my vantage point in the small plane, I look over endless stretches of flat muskeg, broken only by brush and scrub, lonely stands of spruce or willow, and thousands of frozen streams, lakes and ponds. We follow the undulating Rabbitskin River and I see a lonely truck on the thin line that is the winter road.

Half an hour after we leave Fort Good Hope, the radio in the cockpit crackles to life. We are coming in to land at Colville Lake. The pilot visually lines up the aircraft with the snow-covered gravel runway and we land amid softly falling snow. I'm home at last, in the place where my journey with the Dene began in 1971. We taxi up to a small brown hut with a hand-lettered sign — *Welcome to Kah Bah Mi Tue* — and I climb down from the Cessna.

The wall of the Colville Lake airport.

14   Life Today

When I disembark from the plane on the Colville Lake runway for the first time in 45 years, I look around the snowy landscape in wonder. Then I kneel down and kiss the frozen ground. Tears threaten, but I pull myself together. Rising from my kneeling position, I see throngs of people waving at me in the window of the small hut that functions as the airport terminal. Who could they be? I enter the tiny waiting room to find it packed with men, women and children who swarm around me, smiling timidly at the stranger who has come to their community. I don't recognize any of the happy faces.

And then … could this middle-aged woman with long grey hair and glasses possibly be little Helen? Tears are streaming down her face and mine too, as we gasp with joy and embrace each other. That man with thick black hair and a broad grin must be Jean-Marie, now known as Gene. My old friend enfolds me in a bear hug. Helen and Gene are married to each other! They have seven children and eleven grandchildren. Excitedly, we chatter away. So much to talk about! A lot has happened – babies have been born, Elders have passed away, and grandchildren are eager to meet this unusual friend from far away.

My overwhelming feelings are a sense of gratitude and something akin to awe. My Dene companions and I were young together and we have found each other again after almost half a century of following completely different paths. Despite time and distance, those bonds of friendship are still strong, the broken links now restored. I am soon to learn that the entire hamlet of Colville Lake has grown and matured over the years, in a curious parallel with my own growth and maturity.

From the airport, David drives me into town on a wide road with snowbanks on either side. The footpaths of old now run alongside ploughed roads. I am amazed to find that almost every family in Colville Lake owns a vehicle. Trucks, cars, graders and even bulldozers are transported into the community during the few short weeks when the winter road is open. Thanks to the extreme cold every winter, it is possible to scrape an ice road through the otherwise impassable terrain, connecting Colville Lake to Fort Good Hope, Norman Wells, Tulit'a and eventually to Yellowknife. Fuel, oil and cargo are hauled to the Sahtu communities over the winter road during the coldest part of the year.

A raven flies over Our Lady of the Snows church, now surrounded by spruce trees due to the advancement of the tree line.

When Helen and Gene show me around the hamlet, I recognize very little from 1971. Gene now has the only dog team in town. Instead of dog teams, almost every family now owns a snowmobile for winter transportation and an all-terrain vehicle known as a quad for navigating the tundra during the brief summer. Alouie's old cabin, abandoned a few years ago, appears empty and forlorn. Dark windows and sagging boards somehow sadden me.

The church and lodge still stand on the lake shore but now a two-story timber museum towers between the two buildings. Later I learn that the church foundations are crumbling, and the wood stove is a fire hazard.

A twenty-foot pole adorned with dozens of caribou antlers adds a whimsical touch to the lakeside setting.

Where only a few stunted trees grew in 1971, now groves of thirty-foot tall spruce trees stand around the lake and near the airport. David tells me that the water level of the lake has dropped precipitously in recent years. I wonder what caused such a decline in the water level. Animals have changed their habits, too. Muskoxen graze in the vicinity more frequently than in previous years. The winters are so much warmer now that the ice road is only open for three weeks of the year, compared to eight weeks only a few years ago. Worst of all, the vast caribou herd of 1971, estimated at that time to be at least 1.4 million strong, has shrunk to fewer than 4,000 animals.

Perhaps these phenomena are evidence of climate change? The Arctic is a barometer of health for our planet, and the environmental changes that I see today are an alarming contrast with the conditions I observed 45 years ago. Most distressing is the potential impact on the Dene diet – how will the people survive if the caribou disappear?

The settlement itself has changed dramatically. More than 100 people now live here year-round. Power lines supply electricity to homes that are scattered haphazardly along the waterfront. The innovative band leaders plan to introduce solar power[19] to reduce reliance on diesel-fuelled generators. Still, the influence of Dene ancestors permeates every aspect of life in Colville Lake. Joseph Kochon, now the Senior Administrative officer for the Behdzi Ah'da First Nation, shows me a photo of Colville Lake that was taken from the air. The point of land on which the hamlet is situated has the distinctive shape of a caribou head, with the settlement itself located in what would be the eye of the caribou. How could the Dene from centuries ago possibly know what the location looks like when seen from above?

Instead of log cabins and canvas tents, most people in Colville Lake now live in prefabricated houses with indoor plumbing. A water truck fills a large tank in each home and a sewer truck empties the sewage tanks. I am startled to see a 'boil water' advisory posted – is the lake water no longer perfectly safe? I am told that the warning arises from an abundance of caution of the part of the Northwest Territories' regulatory body.

The picturesque mountain across the lake from the hamlet is called Behdzi Ah'da, which means 'place where the caribou go.' The Behdzi Ah'da First Nation band office, located in an Atco trailer, is the vibrant hub of the community. The coffee pot is always on and I can count on finding people of all ages lounging in the reception area. I will stay directly across from the band office in a little log cabin known as the Colville Lake Bed and Breakfast. Complete with a kitchen, bathroom, large common area and four bedrooms, my accommodations are comfortable and cozy. From the entrance to the cabin, I look around the lake at the powder-frosted shoreline forest, entranced by distant shades of azure and grey. I breathe in air

---

[19] In May 2016, Colville Lake launched a unique solar/diesel hybrid system for power, the first of its kind in Canada for an off-grid community.

redolent with spruce and frozen moss. Beyond our tiny outpost lies only vast, impenetrable wilderness. I am in awe.

After I settle into my lodgings, David drives me around the village. The entire tour takes only ten minutes but I am impressed with the changes that have been wrought over my lifetime. The little dirt runway where aircraft landed in 1971 is now a wide, straight road with a few buildings on one side. The replacement runway, located almost a kilometre away from town, is long enough to accommodate relatively large airplanes. The waiting room at the airport is a sturdy building complete with a functioning bathroom.

Everyone in Colville Lake now speaks English! I am amazed that even the youngest boys and girls communicate effortlessly with me. Only the Elders still prefer to speak the Dene language. When we meet up with Johnny Blancho, Helen translates so we can understand each other. Now an Elder, Johnny remembers me very well. He chuckles when he tells the band leaders that Alouie had a crush on me. I can only blush and laugh helplessly. I guess gossip is part of human nature and, as an outsider, I was naturally the subject of gossip. Finally I understand why Alouie's dad didn't like me and why Alouie played so many Dene love songs to me on his guitar. That must be the reason he followed me to Trophy Lodge. Alouie was my friend, but I didn't think of him romantically. Oh dear ... I wonder what else was said about me?

Hand-rolled cigarettes have been replaced with store-bought filter cigarettes which too many people, young and old, smoke regularly. Today's cigarettes are considered by the U.S. Surgeon General to be more harmful than hand-rolled cigarettes fifty years ago, due to the toxic chemicals that are now added to the tobacco. I don't see anyone chewing snuff or smoking a hand-made pipe. Although Colville Lake is ostensibly a 'dry' community, a few people still make their own home brew. Others drink alcohol acquired from bootleggers at an exorbitant price. The burden of alcoholism weighs heavily on this isolated outpost, as it does throughout the Northwest Territories. I soon learn that the concomitant social woes are heartbreaking.

The old trading post at Colville Lake has been repurposed as living quarters for the Co-Op manager.

Where Father Brown had operated a trading post for a few hours each week, now a Co-op grocery store is open for a few hours most days. Closed for lunch and all day Sunday, the little shop is crammed with a very expensive assortment of canned goods and items essential for life in the North. All the stock has been shipped in by air, traveling long distances at great expense. A can of soda pop that sells for $0.50 in Victoria costs $4.25 in Colville Lake. Fresh produce arrives every Wednesday, hauled in from Yellowknife on a DC-3 by family-owned Buffalo Airways. Inevitably, some of the fruit and vegetables are wilted, frost-burned or moldy.

Colville Lake now has a real school with classrooms, resources, accredited teachers and a principal. I smile when I see the sturdy log building, remembering my pitiful attempt to erect a canvas tent where I might teach the children who were so eager and willing to learn from the stranger in their midst.

Technology in Colville Lake is challenging. Connectivity is the first hurdle to overcome. Bandwidth is limited and not everyone has access to the internet. Teenagers scheme to find the password so they can sit outside the band office picking up a signal. Cell service is another headache. Only a select few cell phone companies reach this far into Canada's vast northern interior. My phone doesn't work at all here in Colville Lake. No texting, no phone calls home to speak with loved ones in the south.

Outside the little log cabin, there are still no street signs, no police, no hairdresser, no asphalt, no bank, no department store, no doctor or hospital. When someone in Colville Lake is seriously ill or injured, a plane is summoned to medivac the patient to Inuvik or Yellowknife. Expectant women go to Yellowknife during the last month of pregnancy so that they are sure to have hospital care for the delivery of their baby. A nurse visits occasionally and a dentist comes once or twice a year, mostly to pull teeth.

Without government services, Colville Lake has only limited, intermittent contact with a small number of non-Dene people. The self-sufficient Colville Lake citizens have a well-deserved reputation for entrepreneurship. They prefer to shoulder responsibility for their own community rather than relying on government support. When a new airport runway was needed, the people of Colville Lake took on the challenge themselves. Instead of hiring outside contractors, teenagers learned how to operate heavy equipment. Young and old worked side by side on the project. Despite a steep learning curve on the part of the Colville Lake team, the replacement runway exceeded industry specifications.

Colville Lake people look after each other. Need a haircut? Lacking a barber, folks rely on each other to cut their hair, with excellent results. Men keep their hair cut short. The girls' long thick black hair cascades down to their waists. Need a bank?

The Co-op store performs a few limited financial transactions. The people of Colville Lake and the other Sahtu communities easily adapted to the threat of COVID-19 by dispersing in family units from their hamlets to their temporary homes in the bush.

Many of the people I knew in Colville Lake back in 1971 have passed away. Father Brown had requested burial in the cemetery, and his grave bears the only marble headstone to be seen. The cemetery is much larger now, each neatly-tended plot with its own picket fence and colourful mementoes. Every grave holds a story that I will never know. Seeing headstones with the names of children I had played with in 1971 reawakens fond memories; a wave of grief grips my heart, and I mourn the loss of their souls.

The Dene are patient, measuring time in decades, remembering our summer together vividly despite the passage of so many years. Their spirituality remains strong. Every evening, the people of Colville Lake gather to pray the rosary at the home of an Elder. Many still pray in the Dene language. Young and old never fail to say grace before meals. Every band meeting begins with a prayer. I visit my namesake, Marie Kochon, and read the Bible to her at her request. When Marie passes into the spirit world later that year, I feel grateful for the opportunity to spend time praying with a significant figure from my past.

Every two or three months, a priest visits the community to say Mass, baptize newborns and provide spiritual guidance. In the absence of the priest, the people gather every Sunday morning for their own liturgy in Our Lady of the Snows chapel. Men sit on one side of the church, while women and children sit on the other side. The entire service is conducted by community members, with volunteers stepping up to read aloud from the Sunday missal. Many of the parishioners respond in the Dene language, resulting in a harmonious blend of English and Slavey voices raised up together.

I had spent a summer in Colville Lake and now I am blessed to spend a few winter weeks in the Arctic environment. The snowy scenes are breathtaking... literally. Breathing in the air at forty below means I run the risk of freezing my lungs. Best to zip my down-filled jacket all the way up past my mouth, leaving no exposed skin. Frostbite is a very real possibility. Even appropriately muffled, I inadvertently cough when I first inhale the icy outside air.

Although there is less than an hour of full daylight north of the Arctic Circle at this time of year, the endless golden dawn and lingering purple twilight more than compensate for the lack of direct sunshine. A blanket of snow transforms the entire world into a pure white scene sparkling under the stars. I see the lake gleaming in the moonlight, trees shrouded in white, smoke curling lazily from chimneys, ravens on rooftops, snowmobiles flying past my door. Waves of neon-green Northern Lights mesmerize me as they dance across the dark sky. Yes, Colville Lake has changed in many ways, but the magic remains irresistible, the spell unbroken.

Northern Lights over Colville Lake as seen from David Codzi's front door. Lights of the Co-Op store in the distance. (Photo courtesy of David Codzi, 2020)

The landscape changes with the seasons but the people do not. The Elders still quietly guide communal decision-making. Colville Lake families move fluidly from their bush camps and traplines to town and back again, always retaining their sense of humor and ceaselessly problem-solving. Dene people of all ages are expert at living off the resources of the land, relying on thousands of years of cultural traditions to guide them. The land, the water, the wildlife and the people are all interconnected. The essence of the Dene spirit endures here, untouched by the contemporary world.

Back in 1971, the Dene in Colville Lake relied only on the lake and the land for sustenance and survival. In 2016, their commitment to the environment is still strong, but they now partly depend on outside goods and services. Today, these resilient men and women stand on the threshold of modernity. Indeed, all the communities in the Sahtu are navigating a new frontier. The leaders grapple with legal concerns, mining and mineral rights, self-government, education, health care, social issues and other complex challenges. Still their ingenuity, traditional practices and local skills remain grounded in ancient Dene wisdom.

The little boys who played ball with me almost fifty years ago are now grown men with families of their own and enormous responsibilities. My visit to their community had become part of their childhood memories – baking a cake for the first time, playing ball in the hot sun, learning to speak English in a canvas lean-to. All of them now speak English perfectly. Wilbert is the elected Chief of the Behdzi Ah'da First Nation. Joseph is the Senior Administrative Officer and band manager. Gene runs the gas station and maintains the buildings. Rolly plays guitar and sings so skillfully that his recordings are played on the territorial radio stations. Helen is the office receptionist for Behdzi Ah'da First Nation. When I visit Alouie at his cabin, he pulls a cooked caribou heart from a pot under the sink and offers the delicacy to me as a snack.

Margaret welcomes me back to Father Brown's lodge with a cup of tea, cinnamon rolls and a hearty smile. She is surprisingly eager to chat with me about her late husband. After I left Colville Lake, Margaret and Father Brown entertained European royalty, politicians, movie stars and just plain rich folk from afar. Even Prince Charles visited Bernard Brown and Margaret, seven years after I left them.

Bern Will Brown published a number of books about his life in the Arctic, including *Arctic Journal*, *Free Spirits*, *A Time in the Arctic* and *End-of-Earth People*. I buy the books from Margaret and later discover that Brown's depictions of life in the North do not accurately reflect the Dene perspective. Still, I am grateful for the chance to reminisce with an acquaintance from long ago. (Four years later, in 2020, Margaret passed away peacefully in her Colville Lake home.)

Margaret unlocked the museum in Colville Lake so that I could see the artifacts that Father Brown had collected over more than half a century of living in the North.

Visiting my old friends in their home brings me great joy. Gene and Helen have built a large house for their large family and it's always a beehive of activity. Instead of referring to me by my 1971 name of *Sayday Morie* (younger sister), their children call me 'Auntie' and their grandchildren call me 'Grandma.' I wrestle with the little ones on the living room floor as thinly sliced caribou meat dries above the wood stove. Thin logs suspended a foot from the ceiling run the length of the room. These rails are useful for drying fish and meat and also for hanging snowy outerwear to dry. Gene and Helen and I reminisce about bygone days while nibbling on home-made dry meat and dry fish.

But I've been invited back to this tight-knit community for much more than socializing. David had asked me to conduct an 'assessment' of education in the Sahtu. Like the most visionary leaders, he allows me, as the education specialist, to interpret the term as broadly as needed. To prepare for this task, I had spent many hours developing various strategies for community engagement.

Over the course of those first two weeks in Colville Lake and Fort Good Hope, I quickly learn that one-to-one personal conversations are considerably more fruitful than group gatherings. Invitations to a meeting at the school or band office are often greeted with skepticism by community members. The situation is dramatically different when I talk to the people individually. Everyone is readily forthcoming when I meet them face to face, walking along the road or waiting at the airport for the next flight.

As I walk down the streets of Fort Good Hope or Colville Lake, people of all ages welcome me with a smile, a joke and often a hug. An elderly man with a wizened face and twinkling eyes stretches out his hand and greets me cheerfully, "I've never seen you before!" We chat for twenty minutes before parting, but I never ask his name.

Frequent travel throughout the Sahtu means that I soon know all the North-Wright pilots by their first names. Many of the young men fly around the North for only a couple of seasons before moving up in their career or on to adventures in other parts of the world. Waiting at the airport in each community is an opportunity for me to make new friends and connect with people from throughout the North.

I also face innumerable transportation challenges. One day, my baggage is accidentally offloaded at Fort Good Hope, leaving me without even a toothbrush at my final destination in Norman Wells. Even worse, the documents required for my meetings are also missing. Fortunately, the thoughtful pilots detour to Fort Good Hope the next day to pick up my misplaced luggage. From that day on, I watch carefully whenever the baggage is offloaded along the way to my journey's end.

The Rabbitskin River flows between Fort Good Hope and Colville Lake.

Every time I board a plane, I am transporting personal items from a person in one community to that person's friend or relative in another. Items that I have been responsible for include a goose carcass, frozen trout, dry meat, a tricycle, a set of house keys, an anniversary cake, books, an iPhone cover, bags of clothing, envelopes with important legal documents, backpacks, hockey bags and boxes of goods. Best of all, I am occasionally asked to escort an underage child from their home in one community to family members in another.

The long-ago lesson I had learned that 'the weather is the boss' is still true today. We are at the mercy of the natural elements, especially when it comes to travelling into and out of the Sahtu. Flights are frequently delayed or cancelled due to freezing rain, thunderstorms or a low ceiling. My schedule is invariably disrupted by circumstances beyond my control. Maybe this is why the Dene sometimes hesitate to make time commitments. They know from experience accumulated over generations that elemental forces of nature can change conditions dramatically in an instant. The weather can cause danger on the ground, too. A gust of wind caught me off balance as I disembarked from a small plane during a blustery winter storm one night. I sprained my ankle on the narrow icy metal steps and spent the next two weeks hobbling around the rough northern terrain with only a tensor bandage to support my injured ligaments.

Occasionally, the person scheduled to greet me at the airport doesn't show up. With no taxi service in these tiny communities, I am grateful for the kindness of fellow travellers who never fail to notice my predicament and come to my rescue. I marvel at the nonchalant way that a complete stranger will toss my baggage into his pickup truck and drive me to my destination without expecting any compensation. These generous acts restore my faith in human nature and bring new acquaintances into my life.

Wherever I go in the Sahtu, I meet people who are eager to tell me about life in their part of the world. Elders, leaders, teenagers, parents, children – more than seventy people share with me their ideas for how to improve their communities. With great clarity, the Dene people honestly describe their challenges with regard to education, health care and government policies. They worry about social issues too – alcoholism, drug abuse, domestic violence and even homelessness. When I probe deeper into the general dissatisfaction with the education system, everyone agrees that literacy is a priority because youth need reading, writing and speaking skills if they are to succeed in today's world.

Band leaders and parents are unanimous in their condemnation of the schools, telling me, "The education system has failed our people." Despite well-intentioned teachers, students do not reach expected grade-level standards in their knowledge and skills. Examples abound of youth who are functionally illiterate even after many years of schooling. Sahtu high school graduates who are subsequently tested for entry to post-secondary institutions are found to function at only a grade eight or nine level in most subjects.

Too many students in the Sahtu do not complete high school. Around age 12, many begin dropping out of school. Instead of attending classes, young boys will spend six weeks at a time on their traplines, trapping marten, fox and beavers in the dead of winter. The boys rise early in the darkness, tramp through the snow, set traps, melt snow over a wood stove and sleep in tents even when the temperature outside drops to forty degrees below zero (-14°C). Girls often stay home to look after younger siblings. Others play video games or giggle over YouTube clips.

These activities appeal to young people more than sitting at a desk with a pencil and paper. Yet Indigenous youth are key to our shared future. Young people want to be contributing members of society. They need to be competent in literacy and numeracy in order to make informed decisions when the time comes for them to govern their communities. Indigenous youth can be agents of change in the world. Maybe online learning is the answer?

I quickly discover that there are far too many challenges for one person to implement distance learning in this remote region. Successful digital education requires a complex mix of technology and human skills. Adequate hardware, up-to-date software, sufficient bandwidth and independent study skills are but a few of the factors necessary for successful online learning.

But there are other ways to improve learning outcomes. Maybe the Dene can become creators of knowledge rather than consumers of knowledge. Instead of online learning, we can invite the Dene to tell their own stories that will honour the Dene history, celebrate Dene accomplishments and perhaps establish Dene role models for all Canadians.

With encouragement from the band leaders in the Sahtu, I will do my best to improve literacy skills while also increasing pride in their identity. We agree to find a way for the Dene people to describe the Dene heritage in writing. We will move learning from the classroom to the community. Working collaboratively with young and old, we will publish a book. Maybe I have become the person my younger self had hoped for – someone with the skills and determination to chronicle the true history and spirit of the Dene.

Writing a book is time-consuming and difficult. Add a lack of literacy to the other formidable challenges, and a budding author faces what can be an insurmountable hurdle. This is especially true for Indigenous people who are transitioning from an oral tradition to written language. However, if the Dene can collaborate on a book project, I will compile and edit their writing, then oversee design, publication and distribution of the books.

Perhaps we can accomplish this monumental task by pulling together – Dene thoughts with my skillset. I propose a project that will encourage all Sahtu beneficiaries[20] to write something positive about their Dene role models, traditions and experiences. When we compile the stories, we will have a book that celebrates all things Dene. The band leaders agree to the proposal and we launch the project.

The genesis of the *Dene Hero* Publication Project is my simple quest to understand Dene culture, coupled with David Codzi's vision of including Indigenous contributions to the

---

[20] Beneficiaries are members of the five communities in the Sahtu, as identified in the *Sahtu Dene and Metis Comprehensive Land Claim Agreement.*

curriculum. Under his direction, my fifty-year-old dream of a book providing insights into the Dene of the Sahtu is about to come true. This living history book will not be written by an outsider – it will be written by the people themselves, in their own authentic voices.

Words have the power to change hearts and minds. The Dene use their own words to tell their own stories in the *Dene Heroes of the Sahtu* series. I can't speak for the Dene, but I can stand with them as an ally. I can support their efforts for self-determination. Learning and teaching have formed the core of my life over the past fifty years. It's time for me to share those skills. The Dene have illuminated my life and taught me more than they will ever know. The least I can do now is to give back.

Over the next five years, I travel throughout the Sahtu reaching out to young and old alike. I admit to moments of trepidation, especially upon arriving in a community where I don't know a single soul. But I soon learn that familial ties extend throughout the Sahtu and word of a friendly white woman spreads fast. I am grateful for the opportunity to hear stories, renew connections, meet the relatives of my old friends and learn the true history of the Sahtu from those who have lived it. I am humbled by the depth of the answers to my simple questions, listening in awe to descriptions of lives that stand in sharp contrast with my own.

To date, Indigenous history has been told primarily by fur traders, missionaries and academics. The best way I can think of to truly decolonize the curriculum is to encourage Indigenous Canadians to tell their own stories in their own words. The vision of the Sahtu band leaders is for the Dene to do just that through the *Dene Hero* Publication Project.

As I visit the Sahtu communities, I invite everyone to submit a story, poem, essay, photograph or drawing based on their Dene heritage. Some teachers assign the *Dene Hero* story as part of the requirements for English Language Arts class. Other stories come to me directly from community members. Some Dene authors look to the future; others honour the past.

Young contributors to the book often interview Elders to learn about life as a Dene in bygone years. Others observe people in the community, talk to their families, discuss heroic qualities and then write from their hearts about their Dene identity. Still others take photographs and draw pictures to illustrate the books. Most importantly, everyone is eager to read what they and others have written. All the ideas, stories and drawings are compiled, edited, formatted and published in a four-colour book that is distributed every January at the book launch in each community. My job as Project Director is to work closely with the contributors, listen carefully and scribe their stories if necessary. Edits are made only to adhere to English language writing conventions. I ensure that the words of the Dene authors are recorded exactly as they are spoken or written.

Headquartered in Colville Lake, our project collects stories for the *Dene Hero* books from all the Sahtu communities. Contributors range in age from 10 to 82 years old. The stories, infused with a spirit of strength and determination, honour Dene people, traditions, language, values, culture, spirituality and resourcefulness. Our Colville Lake Youth Team publishes four books in four years, winning the Arctic Inspiration Prize in 2018 for our extraordinary contribution and positive impact in the Arctic. The Prize recognizes northern teams that implement Arctic knowledge for the benefit of all Canadians. We hope that schools will embed project-based learning such as the *Dene Hero* books into the curriculum so that community members have the opportunity to fully collaborate with teachers and students. Working together as allies, Dene and non-Dene can create practical, meaningful projects that benefit Indigenous communities for many years to come.

Accepting the Arctic Inspiration Award for the *Dene Hero* Publication Project in 2018 with Robert Neal, Dakota Orlias and David Codzi.

The *Dene Hero* Publication Project is a way for the Dene to have a presence in history, libraries, classrooms and homes. The books are a source of hope and pride for the Dene of the Sahtu. Indigenous students, band leaders, community members and out-of-school youth write about a person, a spirit, an experience, a tradition, a legend – really, anything that the Dene author feels moved to write about. The books are not for sale in bookstores; instead, they are distributed at joyful celebrations in the Sahtu communities. Rather than being produced for widespread distribution and profit, the books are written by the Dene, about the Dene and for the Dene themselves.

We dream of stocking a library of *Dene Hero* books in every Sahtu home.

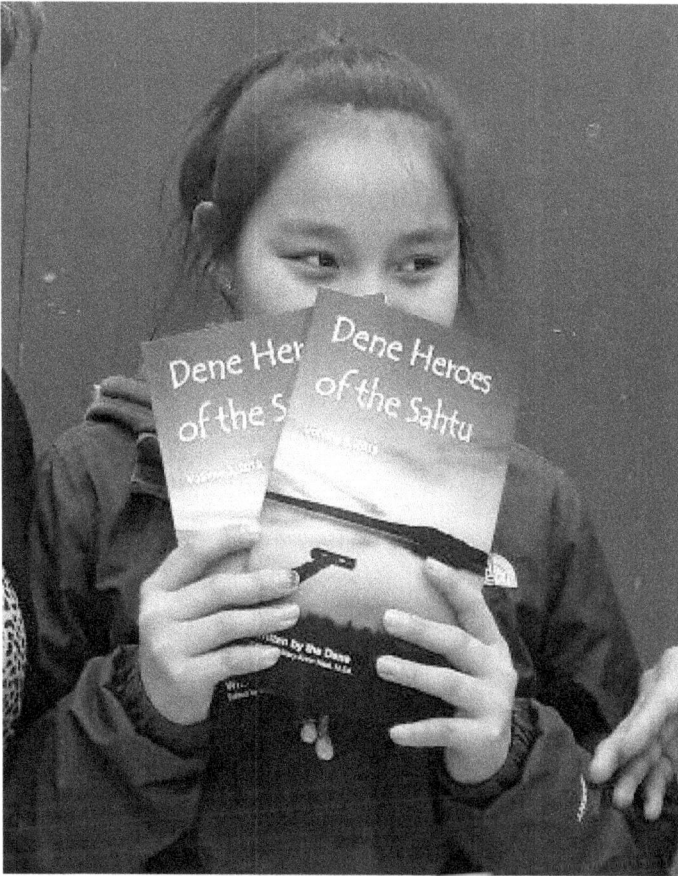

Young Dene authors are thrilled to see their words in print.

The COVID-19 pandemic in 2020 abruptly halted all but essential travel to the Northwest Territories. The policy is necessary to protect public health, especially given the vulnerability of the Indigenous population and the tragic history of entire communities decimated by influenza, pneumonia, tuberculosis and other diseases introduced by settlers. However, the travel ban effectively curtailed the *Dene Hero* Publication Project and other educational initiatives that I had hoped to implement in the Sahtu. Fortunately, the four volumes of books already published remain as an enduring testament to the Dene people.

15   Spiritual Awakening

Sometimes I think our souls can see beyond the reach of mortal cognition. My father used to say that life is a mystery and certainly my life has proved his words to be true. Reflecting on my lived experience illuminates many of the events that happened in my youth, though much remains puzzling. My journey with the Dene, a story shaped in the light of the midnight sun, is but a single strand in the endlessly complex web of life that we share on this planet.

*

At long last, on one of many trips to the Sahtu, I return to Fort Franklin, once again known as Deline, where I had felt a profound spiritual presence fifty years prior. When vast, unfathomable Great Bear Lake comes into view, the tears flow. Stretching to the horizon and beyond, the blue realm holds secrets that remain forever untold. I remember Travis telling me stories of the four Deline prophets; possibly those holy lives are somehow infused into the landscape. Their divine energy might explain the mystical sensations that I experienced on my long-ago visit to the hamlet.

As Armin Geertz, an anthropologist studying the Hopi culture, writes, "Prophecy is a thread in the total fabric of meaning, in the total worldview. In this way, it can be seen as a way of life and of being."

Geertz' words resonate when I listen to the Elders in Deline who continue to observe the message of the prophecies without attempting to explain the specific meaning.

More than 500 people now live in Deline. I am fortunate to visit the community during the annual Spiritual Gathering. The primary focus is prayer, healing, celebration of the Deline prophets and a reminder for everyone in the Sahtu to practice the Dene laws – traditional teachings that focus on sharing, kindness and forgiveness. Leaders, Elders, teenagers, grandparents, men, women and children from surrounding communities also gather in Deline for this popular event. Most come by boat from Tulit'a, Norman Wells and Wrigley, travelling for many hours along the Mackenzie River and then up the Great Bear River to join the festivities on the shores of Great Bear Lake.

I am participating in Deline's Spiritual Gathering because I want to ask the Creator and Dene ancestors to bless our book project and my work with the people. I begin with a visit to the cemetery, where a thirty-foot high white cross, visible for long distances, beckons me. Here I find the same white picket fences and neatly tended plots that lend a quiet beauty to the Colville Lake graveyard. A similar peaceful ambience pervades this lakeshore meadow.

Wandering among the graves, I silently thank the generations of Dene who passed down their wisdom, tenacity and courage to their descendants who inhabit the Sahtu today. My gratitude is tinged with grief for the loss of these ancient souls and their insights which are so badly needed in our planet's current state of affairs.

The belief that all parts of the earth are sentient is deeply embedded in the Dene. As I walk along the path from the cemetery toward the gathering place at the prophet's house in Deline, I recall a story that Travis told me. A few years ago, my friend and his wife escorted an elderly Dene woman from Deline to Yellowknife so that she could visit friends and experience city life for a few days. She had never been to a large centre and everything was new to her.

When they disembarked from the plane, the elderly woman asked what kind of surface she was walking on. This Dene grandmother had never stepped on concrete or asphalt pavement, and the solid blacktop covering the ground was foreign to her. "Oh, that is called pavement," replied Travis, using the English word. His companion looked at the asphalt and scuffed it with her foot. "But it's so hard!" she exclaimed in her own language. "How can Mother Earth breathe?"

A twenty-minute stroll east from the cemetery brings me to the site of Ehtseo Ayah's house. The original catalyst behind Deline's Spiritual Gathering is the legendary prophet and spiritual leader of the Sahtu, *Ehtseo* (grandfather) Louis Ayah, who is widely revered as a visionary. The events begin at Ehtseo Ayah's former home, where worshippers congregate indoors and outdoors. Organizers have created opportunities throughout the weekend for participants to pray individually and collectively. Every evening, fun family events with a moral message take place in the arena.

Most of the Spiritual Gathering activities in Deline take place outdoors, on grassy fields under blue skies, close to the comforting waves of the lake. Men and women of all ages murmur together in groups of two or three. Two teepees lined with spruce boughs invite me to slip inside for quiet contemplation. A cool breeze from the water is restorative.

As I breathe in the fresh air, I am reminded of the ancient Deline legend about *Tudze* (*too d'zay*), Water Heart. According to the legend, Great Bear Lake is connected deep underground to all the rivers, oceans, lakes and waterways around the world. In the depths of the lake beats a giant heart that gives life to our entire planet. This critical life force connecting all living things in our world must be honoured and protected if humanity is to survive.

This drum in Deline depicts *Tudze*, the Water Heart in Great Bear Lake.

The Elders say that Tudze is a gift for all people on earth. The Water Heart will sustain our world as long as humankind respects the ecosystem of Great Bear Lake – its clean water, abundance of life-giving fish and profound impact on surrounding wildlife. Because the lake is a gift for everyone, all people on the planet share an obligation to guard the Water Heart. Determined to honour the words of the prophet, the people of Deline were successful in establishing the Great Bear Lake watershed as the largest UNESCO Biosphere Reserve in North America and the first in the world to be initiated and managed by an Indigenous community. Known as the *Tsa Tue International Biosphere Reserve*, the 2016 agreement is recognized as an international model of how humans can live in harmony with nature.

A hundred years ago, Ehtseo Louis Ayah foretold of a time when hordes of parched and hungry migrants will find their way to Great Bear Lake because it will be the last place on earth with fish and clean water. As climate change looms, Ayah's prophecy seems more and more plausible. We know that all life is interconnected. Scientific research today lends credence to ancient Dene history and legends. For years, non-Dene people scoffed at Dene legends about giant beavers until fossil remains proved the folklore to be true. That is not the first time that ancient myth has meshed with historical fact. Perhaps it is also true that Great Bear Lake will be the last refuge of humanity.

Feeding the fire is a way to release negativity and begin to heal.

My thoughts return to the ceremony at hand. The first important rite is 'feeding the fire,' a communal custom that helps participants let go of grief and trauma. The afternoon ritual is held on the shores of Great Bear Lake beside Ehtseo Ayah's house, where people of all ages gather in a circle around a fire. Each person is encouraged to write a few words

188

from their inmost thoughts on a slip of paper. The subject could be a traumatic incident, a loss or a petition for help. Dene drummers beat rhythmically, praying and singing, as we drop our notes into a basin, along with other mementoes that symbolize letting go. As I release the slip of paper, my heart beats to the tempo of the drums.

Prayers are extended to the north, then the east, then south and finally west, as the offerings are burnt in the fire, a little at a time. Listening to prayers in the Dene language is music to my ears. Intense spiritual energy surrounds the assembly as I participate in this sacred act. Having survived appalling intergenerational trauma, the Dene are recovering their strength and reclaiming their peaceful heritage through healing ceremonies such as this and others conducted on the land. The Catholic bishop who has traveled from Yellowknife to Deline for the occasion delivers a powerful sermon on love and forgiveness. His inspiring words touch the hearts of the listeners.

Later, when Deline Elder Alfred Taneton blesses our *Dene Hero* book project in the Dene language, I recognize one word that he repeats over and over. *Mahsi* (thank you). *Mahsi cho* (thank you very much). Most of his blessing consists of gratitude. He thanks the Creator, the youth, the ancestors, the land, the memories ... he even thanks me for sharing my knowledge and skills with his people. I am humbled.

I wonder whether embracing the Dene philosophy might help humanity begin to heal the damaged relationship between humans, the planet and the Creator. In his 2015 *Laudato Si Encyclical* (*Care for our Common Home*), Pope Francis honoured Indigenous communities around the world for their commitment to the environment. The Pope called attention to the fact that "... for them, land is not a commodity, but rather a gift from God and from their ancestors who rest there, a sacred space with which they need to interact if they are to maintain their identity and values."

Over the years, rationalists such as Rene Descartes and others stripped the natural world of its spiritual qualities, reducing rocks, water, air and plants to the level of inanimate objects. The scientific method does not recognize metaphysical influences. Colonization brought to the New World the concept that our planet is a resource to be used rather than a living entity. Yet who has not gazed in wonder at the beauty of a sunset or rejoiced in a refreshing waterfall? I can whisper my pain to grandfather rock, knowing that my secrets are safe. The life-giving strength of a tree is palpable to anyone who embraces an upright trunk. "Every leaf tells a story," according to the Elders.

James Gustave Speth, an American environmental lawyer and scholar, says, "I used to think that the top environmental problems were biodiversity loss, ecosystem collapse and climate change. I was wrong. The top environmental problems are selfishness, greed and apathy. To deal with these, we need a cultural and spiritual transformation."

Widespread adoption of the Indigenous approach could help effect this transformation and avoid the destruction of our planet. If the environment is perceived as a living being, perhaps humankind will treat 'our common home' with respect.

I reflect on the words of Colville Lake's Chief Wilbert Kochon who told me, "Listen to the land. The land has the answers."

Chief Kochon understands the unspoken wisdom inherent in the land. Perhaps it is time for all of us to listen to the rocks, trees, rivers and animals that populate our world – to learn from and live the Indigenous way of being. The answers to today's complex environmental questions might lie beyond the limits of our present knowledge.

During my week in Deline, I hear about the negative influence of fur traders and missionaries on the Sahtu Dene, and yet the people speak of that history without bitterness. Even the unvarnished truth about Father Brown's abuse of authority, which I am told includes at least one illegitimate child, is stated in a matter-of-fact way. Perhaps the lack of rancour stems from a belief that judgment will come in the afterlife. No need to lay blame while we are still on earth. The Dene wisdom makes sense to me. Certainly their approach to injustice prevents a lot of recrimination.

My dad had often talked about a mine in the Northwest Territories called Eldorado, but I didn't realize that he was referring to Port Radium, the place Travis had told me about when he recounted the story of the German spy who visited Fort Franklin in 1943. Eldorado's mine site at Port Radium was located on the shores of Great Bear Lake. Now I understand why the German spy travelled so far during World War II. He had been searching for clues to the resources required for the atomic bomb that was under development. When I visited Deline again in 2016, I learned the ugly truth about uranium mining and its tragic effects on the men and women of that little community.

High-grade pitchblende ore (now known as uraninite) was discovered near Great Bear Lake in 1930, and Port Radium was established to extract the ore from which radium was refined. Dene men from Deline were hired to carry bags of radioactive ore and load the sacks on to boats. The ore was then transported across Great Bear Lake and down the Great Bear River to the Mackenzie River. The loaded boats followed the Mackenzie River to the Athabasca River, which led to Fort MacMurray. From Fort MacMurray, the valuable ore was transported by rail to southern processing plants in Port Hope, Ontario.

Canadian government publications at the time warned of serious health hazards associated with chronic exposure to the ore. Mining staff who came to Port Radium from the south adhered to strict regulations and were provided with protective gear. The white workers showered before leaving the mine site, and regular blood tests monitored the state of their health. However, Dene workers who were in close contact with the toxic ore were not informed of the risk from exposure to such harmful substances. The Dene men worked without protection, breathing in the highly toxic radioactive dust and often moving the carcinogenic ore with their bare hands.

A world-wide glut of radium and the onset of World War II led to the mine's closure for a few years. Following the splitting of the atom and development of the atomic bomb a few years later, the price of uranium soared. The mine was reopened by the Canadian government, this time to refine the ore for uranium. In 1942, the US government ordered 1000 tons of uranium from the mine at Port Radium on Great Bear Lake. The uranium from the Dene land would be used to build the atomic bombs that were eventually dropped on Hiroshima and Nagasaki, effectively ending the war in the Pacific theatre. Again, Dene men hauled ore in cloth bags without the benefit of protective clothing or showers. When the cloth sacks broke, Dene women used the radioactive fabric to store food and carry supplies, unwittingly endangering themselves and their loved ones.

Many years later, the Deline mine workers began to die of cancer, a disease that was previously unknown to the Dene. The impact on the people of Deline from prolonged exposure to radioactivity is documented in films such as *Village of Widows*, though the federal government has not accepted responsibility for Deline's high death toll from cancer.

The injustices suffered by the Dene at the hands of the mining company are merely the latest in a series of violations that stretches back in North America for more than three centuries. Indeed, Indigenous populations world-wide have been subjected to massive abuses. Environmental degradation, cultural eradication and genocide are the most obvious. Indigenous people have been shunted aside by newcomers who laid claim to their land and their history. Too often, the First People of North America have been resettled next to toxic waste dumps, abandoned to unproductive land and ignored when their water is poisoned and their resources are robbed.

The situation is not as dire in the Sahtu. Dene leaders throughout the Sahtu are determined to have a strong voice in matters that affect their people and their land. On September 1, 2016, Deline beneficiaries celebrated the signing of the *Deline Final Self-Government Agreement*. The Agreement ushers in a new era by creating a governing structure called the Deline Gotine Government which has powers similar to those of a municipal and territorial government combined.

Deline's annual Spiritual Gathering is a time to acknowledge the true history of the Sahtu, address formidable challenges and ask for guidance from Elders and spiritual leaders. I admire the courage of the Dene in the face of questions that I would find overwhelming. But my friends merely chuckle and tell me, "Just keep going." I am determined to do my best to support their goals.

Maybe Be'sha Blondin's words are correct. One day, this tiny, sharp-featured grandmother cornered me at a Dene gathering. I could tell by her piecing gaze that something was on her mind. Looking directly at me with fierce brown eyes, Be'sha asked, "Why are you working so hard for the Dene people?"

Taken aback by the blunt question, I was momentarily flustered. "I'm not sure, Be'sha," I replied honestly. "For some reason, the Dene seem like family to me. What I'm doing is not like work. I feel like I'm just spending time with family members." The elderly woman regarded me intently, looking deep into my eyes. Finally, she said, "That's because you have a Dene heart. You **are** part of our family."

Before I fall asleep in Deline that night, I send prayers of gratitude to the Creator, thanking God for the people and experiences that have shaped the patterns of my life. That journey has been characterized by innumerable coincidences such as the ones described in this book. Though I have stumbled through 69 years with many missteps along the way, I marvel at the synchronicity that has guided me to this place of Arctic energy. Then I dream about the fearless and indomitable Dene people.

As I approach my seventieth year on this planet, I appreciate more than ever my lived experiences – good, bad and indifferent. The memories I call to mind are more than mere recollections of those incidents. They are a displacement of myself in time and space. Events such as the ones described in the preceding pages were witnessed and participated in by my younger self. Then those moments were recalled by my older self. Sometimes I wonder if I am truly the same person, or, as Edgar Allen Poe says, "Is all that we see or seem but a dream within a dream?"

*

A Dream Within a Dream
Edgar Allan Poe 1809 – 1849

Take this kiss upon the brow! And, in parting from you now,
Thus much let me avow: You are not wrong who deem
That my days have been a dream; yet if hope has flown away
In a night, or in a day, in a vision, or in none,
Is it therefore the less gone? All that we see or seem
Is but a dream within a dream.

I stand amid the roar of a surf-tormented shore,
And I hold within my hand grains of the golden sand--
How few! yet how they creep through my fingers to the deep,
While I weep--while I weep! O God! can I not grasp
Them with a tighter clasp? O God! can I not save
One from the pitiless wave? Is all that we see or seem
But a dream within a dream?

16   Afterword

May 15, 2021, marks fifty years since I climbed into the cockpit of a Piper Cherokee headed to Canada's northern frontier. Thus began a journey with the Dene that has lasted a lifetime. I had embraced the unknown and trusted my instincts to venture into a vastly different world. One of the joys of aging is the opportunity to travel back in time, reflect on past experiences and contrast them with the present.

Remember when I played cribbage with Florence and George Barnaby in their little canvas tent in Colville Lake? They now live in Fort Good Hope where the baby boy who swung in his blanket sling above my head is a counsellor with Yamoga[21] Land Corporation.

That little blue suitcase that accompanied me on my teenaged journey? My oldest daughter begged me for it when she moved to Ottawa a few years ago. I haven't seen it since.

The crewcut pilot who escorted me to his cousin's wedding and then flew me to Yellowknife? John went on to become a respected doctor in the United States. Happily married with two adult children, he still loves flying and occasionally visits Canada. We reconnected on Facebook and hope to meet in person again one day.

Young Sharon who was able to pronounce 'orange' correctly during our tent school lesson is now a grandmother and the North-Wright Airways ticket agent for Colville Lake.

Joel and Susan Savishinsky returned to the United States, where Joel earned a doctoral degree, taught anthropology and published a number of books, including *The Trail of the Hare*, based on his research in Colville Lake. Susan became a social worker in Ithaca, New York.

---

[21] Yamoga Land Corporation is named after a legendary Dene hero who saved people by fighting a giant beaver.

My Dene flame from Trophy Lodge? Despite living thousands of kilometres apart, we have, as he had hoped, become 'friends for life.' Over the phone, we share our successes and failures. We laugh about the joys and challenges of family life, talk about politics or the weather, and occasionally reminisce about the olden days in the '70s.

My life partner gives me strength.

And what about me? My freckles are long gone and my once-slender waistline has expanded. As a young adult, I sprawled on the dock at Colville Lake to write about my adventures in a thin coil notebook, and I now sit at a computer in my home office, clacking keys on the keyboard. No longer a naïve, spirited teenager, I am a married university professor with four grown children, concluding a career in education that has taken me to three continents and touched thousands of lives. I have taught in schools, colleges, universities and a maximum-security correctional institution. At conferences and workshops, I have addressed thousands of participants in an effort to convey my understanding of teaching and learning principles. That thirst for social justice remains strong and now is the time to act on my lifelong desire to honour and celebrate the people who are so dear to my heart. Hence this book.

At this point in my life, I have much to be grateful for. I thank all my Sahtu Dene brothers and sisters who challenged me, teased me, told me stories and shared their dry meat, homes, lives and families with me. From 1971 until now, they have nourished my heart and helped me grow as a human being. They have also motivated me to investigate my own heritage.

Dene in the Sahtu trace back their lineage for thousands of years. Meeting folks with such a lengthy ancestry revealed that lack of knowledge in my own identity and sparked a quest in me to learn about my own, pre-settlement ancestry. My father was born in Ireland and both of my mother's parents came from England. To learn about my ancestors, I travelled to Ireland with my youngest son in 2019. In the towns of Ulster, Robbie and I discovered that our forebears had endured poverty, starvation and appalling hardship for centuries at the hands of British colonists. The Irish were forbidden to speak their language or practice their religion. They were forced on pain of death to convert from Catholicism to Anglicism. Marriage to an English citizen was punishable by hanging. Even their traditional dancing was outlawed.

Perhaps painful memories of cultural genocide persist in my DNA; that might explain my affinity for Indigenous people and my indignation at the abuses they continue to suffer. After all, the myth of the 'New World' is a social construct that denied my own heritage as well as the contributions of the original inhabitants of this land. I was taught that I am Canadian, without reference to my lineage. Unaware of my Irish language or culture, I later learned that Irish ancestry was considered by some to be shameful. Irish people were frequently stereotyped as lazy, unwashed drunks. More than once, I was slighted for my ethnic origins. That prejudice might have arisen because the people of Ireland were the Indigenous People in that part of the British Empire.

Indigenous people have rarely been portrayed as role models in popular culture. This, despite the fact that the First People of Canada have played important roles in their communities over thousands of years as leaders, language interpreters, family providers, wilderness survivors, trading partners, historians, cultural guardians and caregivers of the land. Artifacts indicate the presence of the Dene in the Northwest Territories for at least 3,000 years. The Dene Nation claims that they have inhabited their northern territory for 30,000 years.

When Europeans first arrived on the shores of what is now known as North America, the First People of the land taught the newcomers survival skills, shared their food and medicine, and guided the foreigners along rivers, across mountains and through valleys. Present-day Canadians and Americans owe those hospitable human beings a huge debt of gratitude. In addition to their generosity, the Indigenous nature is strong, intelligent, courageous, practical, sensitive, kind and spiritual. That's why I see Indigenous North Americans as true heroes who walk humbly among us.

Many Canadians do not share my views. I have heard stories of overt and systemic racism against Indigenous people around the globe. Stereotypes abound because the colonial legacy – tobacco, alcohol, drugs, processed food, bureaucracy and legal structures – has divided Indigenous Canadians from their traditional nature. Reclaiming their authentic identity is a formidable challenge that requires a concerted effort on behalf of all Canadians. Colonization has also separated us from each other, and that rift between Indigenous and non-Indigenous has widened dramatically over the past 250 years.

My Dene friends tell me shocking accounts of casual discrimination based solely on their appearance. Even the Canadian health care system, purportedly available to all citizens equally, is not immune to prejudice against people of Indigenous ancestry. Here in Canada, years of intergenerational trauma have resulted in staggering inequalities between Indigenous and non-Indigenous Canadians. Indigenous adults are over-represented in prisons, and far too many of their children are in foster homes. The Indigenous population suffers from higher mortality rates, malnutrition, more disease and lower education levels than other Canadians. Many people on First Nation reserves in Canada and Native American reservations in the United States lack access to basic necessities of life such as safe drinking water. All the indicators of poverty are found in Indigenous communities. The relationship with our Indigenous brothers and sisters is badly in need of repair.

Sometimes I wonder how my fellow non-Indigenous Canadians perceive our Indigenous compatriots. For example, if you were to pass Travis on a street, would you see him the way I do? To a stranger's eyes, he looks like any aging Indigenous man with rugged features, missing teeth, wrinkles, bushy eyebrows and grey hair. But to me he is still the strong, handsome and, yes – sexy – Dene man who swept me off my feet so long ago. I know his temperament as a delightful blend of complex character traits. This gentle philosopher is industrious, creative, sensitive, adventurous and humorous, with a heart that beats loyal and true. Hard for a passer-by to see those qualities. Maybe my youthful experience with this remarkable man and our reconnection as adults will encourage readers to look beyond physical appearances to see a soul with a fascinating life story. We are better people when we embrace each other as friends.

The Dene philosophy that I found in the Sahtu can enrich our world immeasurably. This means changing existing policies, procedures and protocols to create more equitable practices and a more compassionate world order. It might also mean that we begin to value wisdom that transcends purely rational, intellectual ways of understanding. Brain research has identified multiple forms of intelligence, including spatial, naturalist, musical, kinesthetic, mathematical and linguistic. Indigenous knowledge might be another form of intelligence that has yet to be categorized.

Dene reverence for the natural world is not unusual compared with other Indigenous cultures. During this time of global pandemic and climate upheaval, the Indigenous voice has never been more important as a way to rethink humanity's role in the world we share with other life forms. Traditional Indigenous skills and cultural practices, integrated with science and technology, could provide the route to human survival. Our broken world needs the Indigenous spirit now more than ever. By that I mean we need imagination, generosity and a different understanding of our place on this planet. It might be possible to protect the environment and forge a better future by creating a global culture that harmonizes with natural systems rather than attempting to dominate nature.

I am forever grateful to the Dene for bearing witness to my adolescent dream of learning about Indigenous ways of knowing and being. I had offered my hand in friendship to a small group of people who live close to the land in an unforgiving environment, and they embraced me as a stranger, accepting without judgment a lost teenager in search of direction. My summer with the Dene in the high Arctic provided a window into some complex mysteries of the human psyche and interpersonal relationships. When I reached out to these men, women and children a lifetime ago, I never guessed that ripples from our bond would stretch half a century into the future. What I experienced in the Sahtu under the light of the midnight sun was a true exchange of hearts. Participating in everyday Dene life changed me and set my life's direction.

In hindsight, my experience with the Dene taught me that it is never too late to take action. The time is always right to tell the truth in love. In the oft-quoted paraphrase of Mahatma

Ghandi's words, "Be the change you wish to see in the world[22]." This book is my response to Gandhi's call for transformation.

Occasionally I regret the years I spent away from the Dene of the Sahtu but perhaps, as Travis says, life is unfolding exactly as it was meant to. I remember my father's words that we are only passing through this life. We need to invest our time wisely. Nothing corporeal is permanent. I will continue to advocate for the Dene, challenge my own assumptions and walk gently in the territory originally inhabited by Indigenous Canadians.

Our Indigenous brothers and sisters can help us understand that we share the world as "our common home," as Pope Francis says. The Dene know that the land, water and indeed all living things are our relatives to be honoured, not resources to be squandered. Dene laws foster moderation, generosity and redistribution of wealth. The Dene consensus system of government patiently listens to all voices in an effort to ensure that everyone agrees to decisions that affect everyone. Learning from the Dene has enriched my life immeasurably.

It is my hope that this story will raise awareness of the quiet courage and dignity inherent in our Indigenous brothers and sisters. Our shared future is uncertain, and hope lies with people of Indigenous descent who have already overcome countless challenges. Maybe readers will embrace the indomitable spirit of the Dene in the Sahtu, a spirit that resides in all Indigenous people. It is time to give credit where credit is due – to the First People of this continent, who have endured centuries of great hardship and are emerging as a force to be reckoned with. We also need to address the wounds in their

---

[22] Gandhi's original words: "If we could change ourselves, the tendencies in the world would also change. As a man changes his own nature, so does the attitude of the world change towards him... We need not wait to see what others do."

Indigenous souls, wounds that will only be healed when our culture forges a real relationship with the First People by acting in solidarity with them.

What now? The future can only be dimly seen; race riots, war, climate change and the COVID-19 pandemic hint at imminent disaster. I don't feel like this is the end of the story. Perhaps the thoughts penned here will be a catalyst to restore respect to an Indigenous population that was shattered by colonization and is now beginning to reclaim its heritage.

I love the Dene and ask readers to recognize the First People of Canada for their heroism and contributions to our society. Over my lifetime and even within the confines of the limited narrative in this memoir, I have experienced different forms of love. I said that I love the Dene, and that feeling is distinct from the way that I love my husband or my children. Still, I must use the same word to describe a decidedly different kind of relationship. Maybe that's not a bad thing. What I know for certain is that love – in all its forms – gives us hope and strength.

*

Ping! A message has arrived on my phone. I look down at the screen and can't help smiling. My old Dene friend has reached out to say hello, for no reason other than to connect. He has spent the day cleaning fish and plucking geese.

Once again, life is good.

*

Questions for Reflection

Book clubs, students and discussion groups might consider different perspectives by contemplating the following questions:

1 **In the Beginning**
   What differences do you see between parenting in the 1970s and parenting today? Why did the author's parents allow her, at age 19, to travel alone to the Northwest Territories?

2 **On My Way**
   "Was I reckless? Inspired? Courageous? Naïve?" Please respond to the author's question.
   Why do you think Father Brown is not happy to see the narrator?

3 **I Arrive**
   What surprises you about the description of Colville Lake in 1971?

4 **Life in a Bush Camp**
   What do you think is missing from the author's description of the tiny Indigenous community?

5 **Trophy Lodge**
   What do you learn about Great Bear Lake in this chapter? Do you agree that place names such as Fort Norman should revert to their original Indigenous names?

6 **My Dene Boyfriend**
   Explain some ways in which the Dene see the world differently than you do.

7 **The Moment**
   Do you detect any undercurrents of tension in the camp? Was it fair to dismiss the narrator from her job?

8 **So This is Civilization**
How might the author's experience of returning to civilization compare with that of Indigenous Canadians who leave their reserves and move to the city?
Name some famous Indigenous Canadians you are already familiar with.

9 **Teaching**
Contrast high school classes today with the description in this chapter.
How are classes today different? How are they the same?

10 **Building a New Life**
How does the author's experience as a single mom affect her perspective on life?
Have you or someone you know experienced struggles similar to the ones described by the author?
Do you agree with the concept of a soul?

11 **We've Been Waiting**
How do you explain the coincidences that led to the author reconnecting with the people in the North?
Were they chance encounters or predestined?

12 **Understanding the Dene**
How have circumstances changed for the people of the Sahtu over the past fifty years?
What steps do you recommend be taken by the band leaders, federal and territorial governments in order to support Indigenous people in accomplishing their goals?
Do you know of other collaborative projects that are similar to the *Dene Hero* Publication Project?

13 **Winds of Change**
How has Yellowknife changed in 45 years?
How has the North remained the same?

14 **Life Today**
   Why do you think Jean-Marie anglicized his name to
   Gene? Contrast his act with communities which revert to
   their original names.

15 **Spiritual Awakening**
   What other spiritual gatherings are you familiar with?

16 **Afterword**
   What do you know about your own ancestry?
   How important is this knowledge to you?

General Questions for Discussion

- What parts of the book strike a chord with you? Why?

- Now that you understand the author's insights into
  unconscious racial prejudice, what are the implications for
  your own life?

- What did you learn about Indigenous ways of knowing
  and being from reading the book? Does the book confirm
  or challenge your existing knowledge?

- When have you observed or been complicit in casual
  racism?

- How reliable are our memories?

Glossary of Terms and Fun Facts

ACTRA – known until 1986 as the Association of Canadian Television and Radio Artists, the organization kept its acronym, which now represents the Alliance of Canadian Cinema, Television and Radio Artists. My number is A02 525.

Arctic Inspiration Prize – recognizes and promotes extraordinary contributions made by teams in gathering Arctic knowledge and implementing this knowledge for the benefit of all Canadians. The Colville Lake Youth Team was awarded the Arctic Inspiration Prize in 2018 for the *Dene Hero*es Publication Project.

Ayoni Keh – Ayoni Keh is the name of the mountain where all the Dene lived in harmony together many thousands of years ago. One day, two brothers shot an owl. They argued bitterly over who had the right to the owl's feathers. This argument split them up, and they parted ways, leading eventually to the dispersal of the Dene in many different parts of North America. Ayoni Keh therefore represents unity among the Dene.

Boreal Forest – also known as the Taiga, this vast region is the world's largest land biome, 50% larger than the Amazonian ecosystem. The boreal forest in northern Canada consists primarily of spruce, tamarack and willow trees.

Bush Camp – Bush has a dual meaning with reference to Colville Lake. The word refers to the ecosystem of spruce, tamarack and willows. It also refers to the isolation, small population of the community and fact that the people derive their livelihood from the land, with limited access to modern amenities.

Colville Lake – originally called *Dela Gotine* (the gathering place), was comprised of people from throughout all four regions of the Sahtu. The lake itself was originally known as *Berah Gutone Tue*, which means 'last found lake.' French fur traders renamed all the lakes in the area. More recently, the Dene began to refer to the settlement as Kah Bah Mi Tue or Kapami Tue [spellings vary] (ptarmigan net lake). Finally, the bush camp was also established as Behdzi Ah'da, as it was a hub for all four area groups when they were on their way to Fort Good Hope. The community is situated in a sheltered bay, which provides some protection from the elements. Most settlements in Canada's Mackenzie River valley are located on the Mackenzie River or one of its tributaries, but the people of Colville Lake are without a direct water route to their settlement. The hamlet can only be reached overland or by small plane. Driving 200 kilometres (120 miles) to the nearest settlement, Fort Good Hope, takes at least four hours on the winter road.

Communication by high-frequency or medium-frequency radio was the only reliable way to communicate with other remote northern communities in 1971. Medium frequency signals are ground waves which stretch a few hundred kilometres. From Colville Lake, Father Brown could reach Norman Wells, Fort Good Hope and Fort Norman. The Roman Catholic priests had their own ground-to-ground channel. The RCMP and Hudson's Bay Company also had their own channels.

Deline means 'where the water flows' in the Dene language. Sir John Franklin and his men lived in Deline for two years on their way to explore the Arctic for a possible Northwest Passage. They renamed the settlement Fort Franklin. In 1993, the community reclaimed its original name of Deline.

Denendeh is the Dene word that refers to the entire Northwest Territories; *Dene Nene* refers to the Sahtu Settlement Land.

Dene Heroes Publication Project was launched in 2016 as a way to preserve history and improve literacy in the Sahtu communities. Four books were published in four years (2017 – 2020). The Colville Lake Youth Team received the Arctic Inspiration Prize of $100,000 CAD in 2018 for the *Dene Hero*es Publication Project.

Dry meat and dry fish – Caribou meat and trout that has been sliced thinly and dried in the sun or over a campfire.

Edmonton Industrial Airport – The airport was known colloquially as the Downtown Airport or the Edmonton Municipal Airport. It was renamed the Edmonton City Centre Airport until it closed in 2013.

Education Beyond Borders – a Canadian non-profit organization dedicated to closing the global education divide through teacher professional development and community education.

Ethel Blondin-Andrew – Born in Tulit'a in 1951, Canada's first Indigenous female Member of Parliament served the Western Arctic constituency from 1988 to 2006.

Fort Good Hope – The traditional name is *Radeyili Koe* [spellings vary], which means where the rapids are. Fort Good Hope was established in 1805 as a fur trading post of the Northwest Company.

Great Bear Lake – Covered in ice and snow for most of the year, this inland sea spans more than 31,000 km² (12,000 square miles). It is larger than Belgium or Massachusetts and deeper than North America's Great Lakes. The dimensions are roughly 320 km (200 miles) long, 175 km (110 miles) wide and 446 m (1463 feet) deep.

Great Slave Lake – The second-largest lake in the Northwest Territories, Great Slave Lake is the deepest lake in North America at 641 m (2014 feet). Copper, gold, nickel, zinc, and lead are mined from the solid rock on the north shore of the lake. Later, I learned that the original inhabitants were called 'slaves' by the fur traders; hence the name 'Great Slave Lake,' is now seen by some as derogatory.

Guardian Angel Prayer – Angel of God, my guardian dear, to whom God's love entrusts me here, ever this night be at my side, to light, to guard, to rule and guide. Amen.

Hitchhiking – Growing up in the 1960s, hitchhiking was a common mode of transport. Along with bellbottom pants and tube tops, we believed everyone should 'make love, not war.' Bad things happened to other people.

Imperial units of measure (eg miles, feet, inches, Fahrenheit, pounds, ounces) – were in use in Canada until the metric system was introduced in the late 1970s.

Indians – The First People of North America were referred to as Indians for the purposes of *The Indian Act* in Canada. The term was in popular usage for hundreds of years. Indigenous Canadians were commonly referred to as 'Indians' or 'natives' until the beginning of the 21st century. Non-Indigenous Canadians were known as 'white.' This terminology reflects the era recorded in the first part of the book.

John Patrick Gillese – Best known as an author and editor, my father also spent his lifetime encouraging emerging authors. In 1961, his short story, *Kirby's Gander,* was renamed *Wings of Chance* and made into the first full-length movie filmed in Canada.

Malcolm Gladwell – In his book, *Outliers*, Gladwell references the '10,000 hours rule,' positing that 10,000 hours of effort are required to become expert in any given field of endeavour. He based his statements on research found in Ericsson, Krampe and Tesch-Romer's *The Role of Deliberate Practice in the Acquisition of Expert Performance*.

Norman Wells – The Dene name is *Tli Gohlini*[23] which means where the oil is. Norman Wells is the first settlement in the Northwest Territories founded on non-renewable resource development.

Northwest Territories – Eleven languages are officially recognized by the government of the Northwest Territories. The Northwest Territories and Nunavut both employ a unique 'consensus' system of government. Democratically elected government officials have no affiliation with a particular political party. Instead of the premier being the leader of a party, the Members of the Legislative Assembly elect a common leader as premier. Nearly twice the size of Texas, the Northwest Territories are home to only 42,000 souls and just 900 kilometres (560 miles) of paved road.

Oblates of Mary Immaculate – Founded in France by Saint Eugene de Mazenod in 1816, the OMI is a missionary religious congregation in the Catholic Church. The Oblates are priests and brothers who are dedicated to serving people in need. Oblate refers to a person who offers his life to God.

Sahtu – The Sahtu is a vibrant hub of resourceful Dene whose culture and values have served them well for thousands of years. An immense territory of majestic beauty, the Sahtu is sometimes called 'the beating heart of the North.' At 283,172 km^2 (109,333 square miles), the region covers almost one-third of Canada's Northwest Territories. The Sahtu is larger than Ecuador, New Zealand or the United Kingdom.

Sahtu Dene and Metis Comprehensive Land Claim Agreement – Signed in 1993, this modern treaty sets out a cooperative resource management regime that requires the

---

[23] Spellings vary

incorporation of Dene knowledge in research and decision-making.

Sahtu Secretariat Incorporated – This organization is tasked with implementing the *Sahtu Dene and Metis Comprehensive Land Claim Agreement*.

Slavey – An adjective referring to a language or to northern Indigenous people. Terms such as 'Slavey' and 'Great Slave Lake' are considered by some Dene to be derogatory because they arose from the early fur traders, who considered the Indigenous inhabitants of the land to be little more than slaves.

Tundra – Tundra consists of small shrubs, grasses, mosses and lichens that can withstand Arctic weather conditions. Arctic lupine, Arctic poppy, caribou moss, bearberry and purple saxifrage are some flowers found on the tundra.

UNESCO Protected Biosphere -- The Tsa Tue Biosphere Reserve encompasses Great Bear Lake and part of its watershed, including the boreal forest that provides habitat for muskoxen, moose, caribou, wolverine, foxes and other wildlife. The Indigenous community of Deline, on the western shore of Great Bear Lake, is defined by its relationship with the lake. The Dene of Deline are the only human residents of the site. The Tsa Tue Biosphere Reserve is the largest in North America and the first in the world to be led by an Indigenous community.

Winter Road – the Mackenzie Valley Winter Road, also known as the ice road, connects all five Sahtu communities for a few weeks every year during the coldest part of winter. The road stretches 1700 kilometres (1056 miles) from Colville Lake to Yellowknife on bumpy, rough ice. Vehicles can rarely travel faster than 50 kilometres per hour (30 mph). Non-essential travel is discouraged due to the perpetual darkness, bitter cold and lack of services.

World View – The Dene world view recognizes that the water, sky, earth, plants and animals are sacred systems that are interconnected and play a critical role for the survival of our species. The Dene have a deep understanding of complex ecosystems, including how to use and manage their sacred resources.

Editorial Notes

As a non-Dene and non-resident in the Sahtu, I have tried to write responsibly and respectfully about the people, the land and the events. I am not an expert and do not attempt to explore sensitive issues in great detail or as an academic researcher; rather, the experiences are recounted from my personal perspective.

In writing and researching this book, I had to make decisions about punctuation, spelling and word choice. Some of the rationale is footnoted in the book. I relied heavily on Gregory Younging's *Elements of Indigenous Style* for guidance. These notes further explain the reasoning behind some of those decisions.

The words 'Indian' or 'native' appear when those terms were commonly used at that time or as found in my primary research document (ie my diary from 1971). The people who originally inhabited the land called Canada are now referred to as Indigenous. Indigenous is capitalized to indicate that it is an adjective derived from a proper noun (eg Canadian).

The original inhabitants of the inland area of the Arctic in northern Canada are the Dene. The word Dene can be an adjective or a noun, singular or plural. It always means person or people. A term such as 'Dene man' is therefore redundant but sometimes necessary for clarity.

The communities of Tulit'a and Deline are referred to as Fort Norman and Fort Franklin respectively, according to common usage at the time. I hope readers are as thrilled as I was when these communities reclaimed their original Dene nomenclature.

The word 'Elder' is capitalized as a sign of respect for the wisdom of older Dene people,

This book does not provide exhaustive details about the Dene because it is merely an effort to capture events that contributed significantly to my personal growth and understanding of the Dene language, culture and philosophy of life. I encourage readers to conduct further research into these remarkable people and their unique environment.

Please forgive any errors or omissions. The information in this book is accurate to the best of my understanding at the time of publication. After 45 years, memories of events and circumstances can vary from person to person and can be interpreted differently; I have tried to faithfully represent the information and ideas that have been shared with me.

I rely on the *Oxford University Style Guide* for guidance on sentence structure, spelling and grammatical constructions but do not adhere strictly to those rules. I employ British spelling over American (eg kilometre, flavour, neighbourhood, colour, traveller).

Linguists refer to the language spoken by the Dene people as Slavey or Athapascan; however, the word 'Slavey' is considered by the Dene to be derogatory, so the preferred term is 'Dene language.'

To replicate my experience, I reveal my understandings as I came to them. For example, I did not know why I was expelled from the camp and only learned 44 years later that it was primarily due to racism.

The names of the Trophy Lodge guides have been changed. A few details have been condensed or summarized for simplicity. Some events have been modified slightly in ways that, I hope, do not change the overall message.

For more information about the Sahtu please see the Glossary of Terms and Fun Facts.

Colville Lake Faces

Thanks to the Prince of Wales Northern Heritage Centre (PWNHC) for bringing back memories of the wonderful people I met in Colville Lake. *Images courtesy of NWT archives/PWNHC.*

NWT Archives/©GNWT PW3/G-1995-001-3476

www.ingramcontent.com/pod-product-compliance
Lightning Source LLC
Chambersburg PA
CBHW062131020426
42335CB00013B/1176